THE MAGIC DOOR

A Study on the Italic Hermetic Tradition

Myth, Magic, and Metamorphosis in the Western Inner Traditions

DAVID PANTANO

THE MAGIC DOOR
DAVID PANTANO
978-0-6484996-4-0
© Manticore Press, Melbourne, Australia, 2019.

All rights reserved, no section of this book may be utilized without permission, except brief quotations, including electronic reproductions without the permission of the copyright holders and publisher. Published in Australia.

Thema Classification:
QYRC (Esoteric Religions), QRYX (Occult Studies), VXW (Occult), QRSL (Roman Religion & Myth), 1QBAR (Ancient Rome)

MANTICORE PRESS
WWW.MANTICORE.PRESS

CONTENTS

Part One

The Golden Bough Initiation   11
Aeneas, the Archetypal Hero of Initiation   13
Orphic Descent Through the River Mnemosyne   16
Indo-European Heritage of Ancient Latium   22

Myths and Symbols of Ancient Rome   25
Sacred Fire of the Vestal Virgins   26
The She-Wolf and the Foundation of Rome   28
Romulus & Remus – Twin Souls of Italy   31
Bachofen on Olympic Virility   33
Heroic Spirit   38
Atavistic Resurgence   39
Italic Tree of Life   43
Ars Italica   44

Origins   47
Return of the Nostoi (Olympians)   47
Schola Italica - Pythagorean School of Italy   48
Underground Pythagorean Basilica of Porta Maggiore   49
Cicero and the Art of Dreaming   52

The Vatic Poets — 55

- Virgil — 55
- Magical Realism in the Roman Empire — 59
- Ovid — 61
- Apuleius and the Art of Metamorphoses — 63
- Apuleius "The God of Socrates" — 64
- Last of the Olympians – Symmachus & Macrobius — 66

Part Two

Middle Ages/Renaissance — 73

- Dante and the Fedeli d'Amore — 73
- Marsilio Ficino on Divine Love — 80
- Pico Della Mirandola and the Christian Cabbala — 83
- Pomponio Leto and the Roman Academy — 85
- Francesco Colonna & the *Hypnerotomachia Poliphili* — 87
- Ludovico Lazzarelli and Giovanni Mercurio Correggio — 91
- Giordano Bruno on the *Sigil of Sigils* — 93
- Cesare Della Riviera on *The Magical World of Heroes* — 101

Appendix

The Practice of Philosophical Ecstasy — 107

Part Three

Post-Renaissance Initiatory Groups — 113

The Magic Door of Rome — 119

- Cagliostro and the Egyptian rite — 132
- Giambattista Vico and Ancient Italic Wisdom — 139
- The Neapolitan School - Domenico Bochini & Giustiniano Lebano — 143
- Giuliano Kremmerz and the Magical Fraternity of Myriam — 148

Appendix

Excerpt from *The Secret World*, Giuliano Kremmerz — 157

Part Four

Contemporary Initiatory Groups   163
    Julius Evola and the UR group   163
    Marco Daffi on the Andromeda Rite   177
    Giammaria and the Body of Peers   184

In Summa   201
    Commentary on the Golden Verses of Pythagoras   205
    On Orphic and Bacchic Initiation   212

Appendix
    The Influence of Giuliano Kremmerz on the UR Group   **215**

Author & Artist Biography   223

figure 1 - Hesperia

part
ONE

THE GOLDEN BOUGH INITIATION

n Roman mythology, the Golden Bough[1] is referred to as a branch with gilded leaves from a tree in the sacred grove that enabled the Trojan hero Aeneas to journey through the underworld safely. The Bough was sacred to Persephone, the queen of the underworld, and associated with the goddess Diana. The legend of Aeneas[2] and the Golden Bough found in the *Aeneid* is a seminal myth of the Western Inner Tradition, as was told by the Roman poet Virgil. Ancient legends tell of lands

---

[1] *The Golden Bough*, by Sir James George Frazer, is the classic study on magic, mythology, and comparative religion. Frazer put forward the concept of the development of human consciousness in stages, with primitive magic supplanted by religion, and religion replaced by science.

[2] Aeneas – a) The son of the goddess of love, Venus, prince of the Dardanian lineage, and one of the few Trojan combatants to survive the Trojan war. Aeneas was designated by poets with the attribute Pius for his devotion and resilience against overwhelming odds to maintain the traditions of his ancestors. In many ways Aeneas exemplifies the Evolian "man among the ruins" for remaining true to the principles of Tradition amidst the chaos of the Kali Yuga.

b) Aeneas can be considered the patron hero of the West because his existential predicament mirrors our own. Aeneas survived a long-standing war, his people were annihilated, his city burned to the ground, and yet he was inspired to start anew in search of the rightful place to establish his roots, which leaves an profound impression on the modern psyche. The Aenean archetype is poignantly relevant to modernity in terms of a quest for identity, self, tradition, and a hearth to establish a future worth living.

to the West known as Hesperia,[3] that follow a trajectory outlined by the evening star Venus. Venus, the goddess of love, mother of Aeneas and benefactor of the Trojans and their descendants, helps her son whenever the gods venture to harm him, creating strife among the gods. According to these legends, the spirit of Anchises, Aeneas' dead father, appears and tells Aeneas that he must visit the underworld, where he will learn what the future holds in store for his people. First, however, Aeneas will have to find the oracle known as the Sibyl of Cumae, who will lead him to the land of the dead. Aeneas locates the oracle, who informs him that he cannot pass through the underworld safely without the Golden Bough. When Aeneas enters the forest to look for the sacred branch, two doves lead him to an oak tree that shelters the bough leading to a portal that descends into the underworld, domicile of the gods, heroes, and demons of Hesperia.

---

[3] Hesperia – a) In Greek mythology, Hesperus. Hesperia (Ancient Greek:"Εσπερος Hesperos) is the Evening Star, the planet Venus in the evening. He is the son of the dawn goddess Eos (Roman Aurora) and is the half-brother of her other son, Phosphorus (also called Eosphorus; the "Morning Star"). Hesperus' Roman equivalent is Vesper (cf. "evening", "supper", "evening star", "west"). Hesperia (Ancient Greek: Ἑσπερια) may also refer to the following characters and places: Hesperia, one of the Hesperides, in some versions (e.g. Pseudo-Apollodorus) is the daughter of Hesperus. Hesperia, is also called Asterope, the wife or desired lover of Aesacus and daughter of the river Cebren.

b) Hesperia is the "western land", the ancient Greek name of Italy, the Iberian Peninsula and Northwest Africa, used in both Ancient Greek and Byzantine sources. *Bucolics, Aeneid, and Georgics of Virgil* (Ginn & Co). *Litus in Hesperium; quaerit pars semina flammae* (Lit. A shore in Hesperia [Italy], one of them seeks the seeds of flame).

Aeneas, the Archetypal Hero of Initiation

Pius Aeneas embodies the perfect type of Roman. He is our point of reference and represents the paradigmatic model of the Dardanian lineage. The operations that form part of his initiation pertain to the Orphic-Pythagorean tradition and furnish proof of the Roman and Italic (and non-Italiot) legitimacy of Pythagoreanism.[4]

The Golden Bough myth recounted by Virgil outlines the key parameters of a branch of initiation, endemic to a specific people, who later formed the nucleus of the Roman tradition. This form of initiation, when stripped of its external vestiges and reduced to its essence, outlines a path to reclaim an identity of self and tradition.[5] The same themes manifest throughout the wheel of time and correspond to the cycles of life, death, and rebirth.

They tell of a past Golden Age, an uprooted tree of life, of long wars, invasions, and a civilization in decline. In summary, of an alienation from the perennial tradition which Giordano Bruno states has become a 'sickly tree spouting blood and an abandoned stump sterile for a

---

[4] Sebastiano Recupero, *Amor*, Furnari, 1990.

[5] Aeneas' journey to seek out his identity and homeland is articulated through the many myths and legends that recount Aeneas' story. The devastation of his former homeland (Troy), the struggle to surreptitiously carry his family and sacred relics (palladium) out of Troy and search for a new homeland to establish his altar, outlines the complete journey of integrating the self in tradition. Aeneas does not search for a new land, rather he searches for his lost homeland, where he can live in peace and his descendants can thrive. This is confirmed in the *Aeneid*, when Dido, the queen of Carthage, asks Aeneas where he is headed towards and Aeneas is quick to answer:

I'm looking for my Homeland, Italy,
The cradle of my race
Descent from the highest Jupiter.

THE MAGIC DOOR

figure 2 – Aeneas

millennia.'[6] These legends also foretell a future cycle of rebirth and resurgence that will usher in a new Golden Age, led by intrepid beings whom the ancient sages describe as an intermediary between humans and the divine – the Heroes.[7]

In today's terms what meaning could the Golden Bough bestow upon men? What can we learn from a quest that promises safe passage through the underworld for those worthy of such a pursuit? What relationship does today's man have with the transcendent, the spiritual, and the divine?

---

[6] Giordano Bruno, *The Heroic Frenzies* (translation by Paulo Eugene Memmo, Jr.), Second Dialogue: "Here, then, is how he is dead though living, and alive while dying; as when he says, I endure a living death and a dead life. He is not dead, because he lives in the object, he is not alive, because he is dead to himself; he is deprived of death, because he nurtures thoughts in the object; he is deprived of life, because in himself he neither can vegetate nor sense anything. Besides, he is most base when he considers the loftiness of the intelligible object and realizes the weakness of his power. He is most lofty through the aspiration of the heroic desire that carries him far above the limit of his own nature, most lofty through the intellectual appetite whose operation and design is not to join his desire to its object; and he is most base because of the violence brought upon him by the contrary sensuality weighing down toward the inferno."

[7] Heroes – in Classical Graeco-Roman mythology, the hero is often associated with divine ancestry, and endowed with great courage and strength, celebrated for his or her bold exploits, and favored by the gods. The eminent Hungarian classicist, Karoly Kerenyi, describes this: "The hero, as meets us in legend assuredly embodies, even more than the gods of the Greeks, a teaching concerning mankind. His purely human characterization is fully possible, for which the divine is the datum serving as the starting point, we may term the divine, with the word 'glory', 'radiance', or 'splendor'. The glory of the divine, which falls upon the figure of the hero, is strangely combined with the shadow of mortality." C. Kerenyi, *The Heroes of the Greeks*, Thames and Hudson, 1959, pg.3.

Orphic Descent Through the River Mnemosyne

In the Orphic tradition, initiates were taught a technique to drink from Mnemosyne, the underground river of memory, to purify consciousness through a process of sublimation and find their true self, thus terminating the endless transmigrations of the soul. This tradition was imparted to the Aeneades, the descendants of Aeneas, to follow a path of light towards the western star (Venus) and revive the lands of Hesperia. The path in search of the lost realm begins internally with the excavation of the Self and the centering of consciousness at the base of the self, in the soul (*Numen*).[8]

At the core of the Golden Bough myth is an Orphic-Pythagorean initiation that concerns the initiate's spiritual rebirth and transformation.[9] The initiation reconfigures the soul by a process of sublimation through the internalization, detachment, and distillation of consciousness centered at the Self (*Materia Prima*). Consciousness rooted at the ontological ground of being prefigures a *metanoia*[10] or great transfiguration of the

---

[8] Numen – The ancient Roman term for the soul, source, and transpersonal essence of being. The Numen, in an experiential context, is the irreducible primal root of consciousness. In Hermeticism the Numen (soul) is characterized as the monad or numenal root that integrates the matrix of elements: Air (Aeria or vital forces) with Fire (Ignis or consciousness) and residing within the ethereal repository (Aether or space) of ultimate reality.

[9] Orphic Initiation – Fritz Graf and Sarah Iles Johnston, *Ritual Texts for the Afterlife: Orpheus and the Bacchic Gold Tablets* (Routledge, 2007). Ana Isabel Jimenez San Crist, *Instructions for the Netherworld: The Orphic Gold Tablets* (Alberto Bernabe, Brill, 2008).

[10] Metanoia – A classical Greek term (μετάνοια) for an inner transformation, a change in spiritual orientation, a transformational change of heart, or a spiritual conversion. Greek source: "from *metanoiein* to change one's mind."

matrical elements of the Soul[11] by empowering the Ignis (fire) principle and corresponding powers.[12]

The initiatic practice of cultivating the Fire element transforms the psyche and its mind streams with amphibian-like attributes, on land (phenomenal) and in sea (astral) to heighten consciousness with prodigious powers of awareness and imagination, represented symbolically by the winged feet of Hermes,[13] that project

---

[11] Elements of the Soul – These are the primary extension of being via the principle of the soul as four elements. The elements refer to the classical world's understanding of the four constituent components at the core of universal being outlined by Aristotle and other ancient Greek philosophers. According to ancient Greek philosophy, the theory refers to the belief that the universe is comprised of four "elements" (Plato, 375 BC) or "roots" (Empedocles, 445 BC), namely a tetradic or quarternary of four elements: earth, air, water, and fire. Aristotle added a fifth element, aether, which is also known as *akasha* in India and quintessence in Europe. The concept of the pentadic or quinary of five elements formed a basis of analysis in both Hinduism and Buddhism. In Hinduism, particularly in an esoteric context, the four states-of-matter describe matter, and a fifth element describes that which was beyond the material world (soul). W.K.C. Guthrie, *A History of Greek Philosophy, The Earlier Presocratics and Pythagoreans* (Cambridge).

[12] Fire Element – Avicenna, *Cannon of Medicine* (1999), pg.16– Avicenna (Ibn Sina). The natural position of Fire is above all the other elements and it matures, rarefies, refines, and intermingles with all things. Its penetrative power enables it to traverse Air. With this power it subsumes the two heavy cold elements (water, earth) and by this it keeps the elementary properties in harmony. It is that which expands, rises, and moves towards outer limits. Any substance that is highly reactive or catalytic in nature is predominantly fire.

Giuliano Kremmerz, *Opera Omnia iv*, pp.170-171: "The fire of love is the first fire of Gnosis (identification with light). Spirit and breath, are one fire that chemically transmutes heavy matter into ethereal matter. The word *spiritus* contains the radical, *Pir* which means fire, and blazing fire at that, it is by means of this fire of love that the angel Uriel transforms …." Giovanni Pontano, *Letter on Philosophical Fire*, refers to Celestial and Philosophical Fire.

[13] Hermes is described adorned with wings on his sandals and

externally through somatic frames or internally through astral streams – dreams, visions, imagination, etc. Inspiration, whether in the form of ideas, insights, dreams, or transcendent visions are the internal manifestations of spiritual forces. As lord of the inner and outer realms, the initiatic hero operates from a greater base of freedom by integrating capacities gained internally with those externally to integrate with a broader and deeper dimension of the Self.[14]

---

therefore was the fastest of all Greek gods. Because of his speed, Hermes received the role of the messenger and conductor of souls to the Underworld. According to legend, Hermes was the only Olympian god who was authorized to visit Heaven, Earth, and also the Underworld. Hermes star or celestial light is referred to in the literature of Hermeticism as the comet, meteor or shooting star, *The Book of AK Z UR*.

[14] Self - Refers to the transcendental 'I' that is the conscious vector enucleated at the core of being that precedes expression into the personal self. The realization of consciousness of the Self is referred to in the literature of Hermeticism as the Fixed Star (Stella Fissa). In alchemy the root of being is the first nature (Materia Prima) of the self. The soul is the individualized source of consciousness.

Fixed Star – Marco Daffi, *The Avatars* (Gli Avatars),

"... in person (Kremmerz) told me, much more, and especially that which he hypothesized, almost ironically, concerning the acquiring of a capability or what should be acquired as soon as one attains the so-called Fixed Star state or state in which the vital energy manifests from the fifth element (beyond the four bodies) of being and becomes a fluidic body (Hermes wings) that subtly encapsulates the four elements, so that these, in post-mortem, do not lack a common connection (ligament, branch) but enter, thus, in a relative state of quiescence or inertia. Moreover, even in an existential context, the constitution of the Self's higher bodies, the spiritual (solar) and the intellective (mercurial), nucleated at the center of the cross (Self's matrix) of an individual both in a manifested and occulted sense, from fixed becomes mobile. In this way they form what the alchemists call the lamp (*ampoulle*), that is, a complex of vital energy that creates a formative and intermediary medium of the two bodies that constitute the true psychic activities and assumes in itself the potential virtues of the two lower bodies. In this way, in the Hyliac plane of manifestation

The initiatic hero undergoes a transformation of consciousness that radically reorientates his sense of identity. This internal form of metamorphosis transcends ordinary spatial and temporal thresholds to open inner channels that facilitate the reception of spiritual forces like those rendered by Aeneas in the Golden Bough myth. Understood from an initiatic perspective, the Golden Bough functions as an instrument or branch to connect the leaf (individual soul) with the trunk (spiritual tradition). Traditional societies are by nature oriented towards sacred dimensions, whereby sacralised objects—art, architecture, literature, historical or religious figures—are invested with qualities that are conducive to connecting the individual leaf with the tribal trunk. The opening of spiritual channels impart the initiatic hero with internally experienced reference points (*anamnesis*) to identify with the nature of the Self and the spiritual forces that feed into the soul. The Golden Bough *katabasis* sublimates consciousness to a deep seated and transcendent void at the center of being by purging the psyche of profane attachments and eradicating extraneous chains of identification (beliefs).

In the ancient Indus valley, the Āryas or nobles, refer to the individual who realizes an inner state of liberation as *jivamukti*[15] and describe this state in terms of a deep awareness, where one who sees the void and affirms the core of being through the exigence of conscious vehicles –

the Self's matrix or quaternary of elements (solar, mercurial, lunar, saturnian) remain connected, and in an alternative astral or occult plane or in the post-mortem they form a virtual quaternary which retains consciousness, the faculty of perception, manifestation, and even enhances it."

[15] Jivamukti – Yogic term referring to an individual state that is liberated from existential conditioning. A state where consciousness is integrated with the soul (*Atman*). George Feuerstein, *The Deeper Dimension of Yoga*, Shambhala Press, 2003. Mircea Eliade, *Yoga Immortality and Freedom*, Princeton University Press, 1958.

ideas, emotions, and actions. In this liberated state, where consciousness is not attached to objects, the symbolic force of the ritual operates as semiotic vectors to seed the initiate's unconscious substratum with spiritual influences affiliated with the archetypes of the tribe.

Consciousness $\triangle$ sublimates when it internalizes and separates from $\triangle + \text{-} \nabla$ somatic influences, purifies when detached from lunar influences $\triangle + \text{-} \nabla + \text{-} \nabla$ and rarefies by the integration of the life force ($\triangle +$) with purified consciousness ($-\triangle + \text{-} \nabla + \text{-} \nabla$) to transform the initiate's inner-self into *noumena* ($* + \text{-} \triangle + \text{-} \triangle + \text{-} \nabla + \text{-} \nabla +$) that can arouse intense enstatic states which manifest as the inner experience of spiritual forces.[16] Internally perceived noumena occur as a result of the transposition of spiritual forces through archetypal forms which manifest in metaphoric representations. Similar to the Golden Bough ritual where the gift of foretelling the future of the Dardanian *stirpes* is transmitted to Aeneas by Persephone, the rituals are performed to receive influences from the sidereal luminaries and thus seed the initiatic hero with requisite Olympian virtues[17]

---

[16] Kundalini – Represents the arousal, integration, channeling, and expansion of life force energy with consciousness.

Swami Satyananda Saraswati, *Kundalini Tantra*, Bihar School of Yoga, 1984. David Gordon White, *The Alchemical Body, Siddha Traditions in Medieval India*, University of Chicago Press, 1996. Shyam Sundar Goswami, *Layayoga: The Definitive Guide to the Chakras and Kundalini*, Inner Traditions International, 1999.

[17] Seven Divine Virtues – Refers to the constellation of sidereal effluvia that operate as vertically tangential vectors of internal forces and individuated with distinct attributes. The seven classical planets are those easily seen by the naked eye, and were thus known to ancient astrologers as the Sun, Moon, Mercury, Venus, Mars, Jupiter, and Saturn. Sometimes, the Sun and Moon were referred to as "the lights" or the "luminaries". Astrologers call the seven classical planets "the seven personal and social planets", because they are said to represent the basic human drives of every individual. The personal planets are

attributed to Apollo (Sol), Diana (Luna), Mars, Venus, Jupiter (Jovis), Mercury, and Saturn as well as those associated with the *telluric* (Vesta) and *chthonian* cults.

Seen through the lens of practical initiation: *Magic is understood as the application of inspired imagination, or more precisely as the application of spiritual forces arising from the Numen through the imagination in the form of inspirations, insights, intuitions, etc. and projected outwards across causal, astral, and phenomenal dimensions.*

The magical act is conceived internally by spiritual inspirations and executed externally through the imagination. However, it should be clearly understood that not all imaginative acts are magical acts. For example, the exercise of self projections arising merely from intellectual or sense stimulated sources, however successful the desired outcomes may be, are not magical acts for they lack the requisite spiritual components, and are constrained by selfish and somatic-centred frames of reference. The word 'magic' is related to the ancient Iranian root-verb 'to make' and the consciously inspired application of spiritual knowledge and wisdom.

The internal transformations undertaken by the Aeneadean katabasis correlate with Atavistic forms of initiation particular to cultures with deep rooted

the Sun, Moon, Mercury, Venus, and Mars. Jupiter and Saturn are often called the first of the "transpersonal" or "transcendent" planets as they represent a transition from the inner personal planets to the outer modern, impersonal planets. The following lists the planets and their associated characteristics:

- Saturn: rootedness, depth, melancholy, and tranquility
- Jupiter: governance, industriousness, and hunting
- Mars: soldiering, will, and warfare
- Sun: projection, light, insemination, music, and athleticism
- Moon: purity, creation, birth, reception, and tenderness
- Mercury: prudence, craftiness, communications, and commerce
- Venus: amorousness, and passion

traditions of ancestral veneration. Seen from a higher purview, the hero is qualitatively lord of both the inner and outer realms, self determined and autonomous with an adamantine nucleus of being (Numen, fixed star). Articulated in Homeric and Hesiodic terms, the hero represents virtue, duty, and simplicity.

As exemplified by the Roman patrician, Lucius Quinctius Cincinnatus (519–430 BC), who despite his advanced age, worked on his small farm until an invasion from the neighboring Aequi tribe, prompted his fellow citizens to call on him to take charge of the state. He abandoned his plough to assume leadership over a militia of tribal members and achieved a swift victory over the Aequi, but was also quick to relinquish his power once the battle was over and returned to work on his farm. His successful military enterprise and rapid resignation of near-absolute authority at the end of the crisis (traditionally dated as 458 BC) are often cited as examples of heroics; self-sacrifice, service to the good, civic virtue, subordinated personal ambition, and modesty.[18]

The Indo-European Heritage of Ancient Latium[19]

Pioneering research was conducted over the better part of the last century by Georges Dumézil and Émile Benveniste, who contributed to rewriting the narrative concerning the earliest known Indo-Europeans. Around the middle Neolithic (circa 5500-4500 BC), the Proto-Indo-Europeans appear as nomadic people who originated from the Eurasian steppes, near the northern Caucasus

---

[18] Lucius Quinctius Cincinnatus, Titus Livy, *History of Rome*, Penguin Books, Book 3.

[19] Latins, Indo-European tribes – https://en.wikipedia.org/wiki/Latins_(Italic_tribe)

region of central Asia. Their livelihood was centered around horses and cattle herding. During historical times, the same socio-cultural lifestyle was maintained by people descended from the Indo-Europeans, who were known to the Greco-Romans as Scythians, and whose languages belonged to the Iranian root. Based on the common cultures of the various Indo-European peoples in the historical era, scholars have reconstructed elements of Proto-Indo-European culture. Relics of such elements have been noted in Roman and Latin customs. Examples include the following:

- The kingship-system of the Indo-Europeans is considered by anthropologists to best fit a patrilineal society, in which descent is recognized through the father's line and spouses are taken from outside the kingship-group.
- A supreme sky-god: The chief god of the Indo-Europeans was a male sky-god, known as "Father Sky", from which descends the principal Latin god, Jupiter, derived from the archaic "Dieus-Pater" ("Sky-Father"). Indo-European tribes also venerated a god of thunder and lightning. Among the Latins, this deity appears to have merged with the sky-god, and as is ascribed with the power to hurl thunderbolts. Jupiter is also associated with the epithets Jupiter Tonitrans ("Jupiter the Thunderer"), Jupiter Pluvius ("Jupiter the Rainmaker"), and Jupiter Fulgurator ("Jupiter the Thunderbolt").
- Fire-worship: A central feature of life was the domestic hearth. The Indo-Europeans are known to have consecrated fire in their religious customs. The best-known example is the fire-worship of the ancient Iranian religion of Zoroastrianism. The

Romans kept a sacred fire burning in the Temple of Vesta, in honor of the goddess of the hearth.

MYTHS & SYMBOLS OF ANCIENT ROME

Mythology is the idiom through which archetypes manifest and the form by which the spiritual forces affiliated to the tribe are revealed. Myths are by definition, atemporal and aspatial, they transcend historical and biographical parameters to represent the perennial values encoded within the tradition of the tribe.[20]

The two symbols most often associated with the Roman tradition are the eternal flame guarded by priestesses devoted to Vesta (the deity of the hearth) and the She-Wolf suckling the twin infants, Romulus and Remus, the founding fathers of Rome.

---

[20] Myths are the language through which archetypes are expressed. Likewise, in a broader purview, heroes are the expression and synthesis of ascending tellurian forces and descending sidereal forces. This is similar to the meaning Ezra Pound prescribed to poetry, "myths are news that stays news." Myths are invisible to the external senses yet remain forever present to the internal senses. They have a protean nature that provides perpetual meaning and significance regardless of time and place.

Sacred Fire of the Vestal Virgins[21]

One of the most celebrated and enduring rituals of the ancient world was the consecration of a perpetual flame to the presiding deity of the hearth in ancient Rome. The fire of Vesta was a flame kept illuminated on an altar located near to the center of Rome and attended by a college of priestesses – Vestal Virgins. They tended to the sacred fire and performed the requisite rituals connected to domestic life. There were six priestesses in number, selected by lot ,and each served for thirty years. By analogy, the Vestal Virgins also contributed to the purification of the city through the consecration of the sacred rituals, which were renewed every year on the Kalends of March (seventeen). The priestesses were sworn to a vow of chastity to ensure that their inner purity was transferred through the exercise of rituals and augured auspicious outcomes. The Vestal Virgins attended to maintaining the perpetual flame of the sacred fire and by this hieratic act guarded the eternal life of the Omphalos or inner center of the realm, to ensure that Rome remained Aeternitas Romae.

> The union of the four elements forms the fifth essence, the root of the moon and the sun – Louis Cattiaux, *Le message retrouvé.*

Understood through the lens of alchemical operations, the sacred flame tethered to a hearth symbolizes an inner vector (heroic) ascending upwards. In the archaic Roman tradition, the sacred flame (Ignis) connotes both collectively and individually the same properties of consciousness, illumination, rarefaction, ascension, and

---

[21] Vestal Virgins and the Sacred fire of Vesta – *Etude sur Les Vestales d'apres les classiques et les decouvertes du forum par L'Abbe Elisee lazaire*, Pardes/Guy Tredaniel. Collection Rebis, 1986.

transcendence.[22] The Latin word Ignis is cognate with the Sanskrit Agni, both refer to fire and derive from the same Proto-Indo-European linguistic root.[23] Within the classical myths of the Western tradition, Prometheus epitomizes the Titanic[24] misappropriation of fire by stealing the sacred flame from the gods. He paid dearly for this act of *hubris*, until—and it is significant to note the underlying symbolism—the Titan Prometheus was freed by the Olympian hero *par excellence*, Heracles.

In the Oriental traditions, and especially within the Tantric practices of Yantras and Mantras, esoteric techniques are incorporated to activate conscious energy through structures that channel vibrational currents (*Vayus*) vertically to the higher centers of the subtle body. Symbolically, △ (the sacred flame) represents the

---

[22] The sacred fire of Hermeticism refers to the whitening of Latona, where the base matrix of the Self is purified to the point of reaching a state of perfection (Self realization) in the manner of Gold. Transposed onto a spiritual level, the flame represents the heroic spirit pillared in the human form and fueled by an inner combustion that ascends upwards in a leap to the divine.

[23] Agni – In the classical cosmology of the Indian religions, Agni as fire is one of the five constituents (*Dhatus*) along with space (Akasha/Dyaus), water *(Jal)*, air (*Vayu/Varuna*) and earth (*Prithvi*), the five combining to form the empirically perceived material existence (*Prakriti*).

[24] Prometheus is a Titan, who defies the gods by stealing fire and giving it to humanity, an act that enabled progress and civilization. Prometheus is known for his intelligence and as a champion of mankind. The immortal Prometheus was bound to a rock, where each day an eagle, the emblem of Zeus, was sent to feed on his liver (in ancient Greece, the liver was often thought to be the seat of human emotions), which would then grow back overnight to be eaten again the next day. In some legends, Prometheus is freed at last by the hero Heracles (Hercules). The banishment of the warring Titans by the Olympians to the chthonic depths of Tartarus was documented as early as Homer's *Iliad* and the *Odyssey* where they are also identified as the *hypotartarioi*, or, the "subterranean."

equilateral triangle where the horizontal plane at the base supports the vortex rising perpendicularly from the meridian. This aspect of harnessing internal energies is represented by yogins assuming the *Padmasana* position (lotus) in deep meditation, where the central nervous system coils vertically around the spine and functions as an antenna to channel conscious energy downward ▽ to the somatic level and inversely to raise consciously-fused pranic energy upwards △ through the vehicle of *Kundalini* vibrations towards spiritual freedom ࿎.

The She-Wolf and the Foundation of Rome

In ancient Latium,[25] the myth of the She-Wolf suckling the abandoned twin-babies, Romulus and Remus, is closely associated with the legendary founding of Rome. Traditional sources attribute the date of Rome's founding to April 21, 753 BC by the brothers who, through royal birth, were the titular heads of the three major tribes of primitive Latium. The tribes were comprised of the major ethnic groups that made up ancient Rome. The Ramnes were of Latin (Indo-European) stock, the Tities represented the Sabines (indigenous Italic tribes), and the Luceres were Etruscans (a mixture of Indo-Europeans and non-Indo-Europeans). According to ancient legends, the brothers Romulus and Remus were recognized as the legitimate descendants of Aeneas, whose fate-driven journey to return to the kingdom of his ancestors, Italy, was described by Virgil in *The Aeneid*. The Etruscans[26] were of Tyrrhenian stock (non-Greek). Tyrrhenian was

---

[25] Latium is the territory surrounding Rome that included Alba Longa, where ancient legends attest Aeneas was destined to set up his kingdom and continue the Dardanian lineage.

[26] Etruscans – There are scholars, including Nancy Sandars, Michael

figure 3 - Romulus

the Greek name for the Etruscans, and although there is no definitive attribution concerning their exact origins or formation, one theory that still carries water suggests that the progenitors of the Etruscans originally migrated from Lydia, along the North-Western Aegean coast of Anatolia, shortly after the fall of Troy c. 1250 BC.

The origins of ancient Rome's foundation myth are subject to ongoing debate. The founding inhabitants may have derived their myths from Latium's own indigenous tribes. Legends recall that the twins, Romulus and Remus, set out to build a city of their own and disagreed over which hill to build their city on. Romulus preferred the Palatine Hill, above the Lupercal; Remus preferred the Aventine Hill. When they could not resolve the dispute, they agreed to seek the god's approval through a contest of augury. Remus first saw six auspicious birds but soon afterward, Romulus saw twelve, and claimed to have won divine approval. The dispute furthered the contention between them and resulted in a battle that ended with Romulus killing Remus. As oral history would have us believe, Romulus went on to build the city of Rome, its

---

Wood, and Eberhard Zangger, who hypothesize that the Teresh are the same people as the Tyrsenians. The Teresh are an ethnic group listed among the Sea Peoples based on later Egyptian sources. The Sea Peoples are a purported seafaring confederation that attacked ancient Egypt and other regions of the East Mediterranean prior to and during the Late Bronze Age collapse (1200–900 BC) who appear in a number of Egyptian inscriptions from 1200-1150 BC. A famous passage from Herodotus portrays the wandering and migration of Lydians from Anatolia because of famine:

> In the days of Atys, the son of Manes, there was a great scarcity through the whole land of Lydia ... So the king determined to divide the nation in half ... the one to stay, the other to leave the land. ... the emigrants should have his son Tyrrhenus for their leader ... they went down to Smyrna, and built themselves ships ... after sailing past many countries they came to Umbria ... and called themselves ... Tyrrhenians.

institutions, government, military and religious traditions and reigned for many years as Rome's first king.

Romulus & Remus – Twin Souls of Italy

The Mediterranean or middle earth, as the name suggests, is at the crossroads between various peoples with different traditions and spiritual orientations. Italy lying at the center of the Mediterranean has been, and continues to be, a land that receives and absorbs many different and divergent strands of traditions that derive from the four cardinal directions.

The archaic Roman[27] is often characterized by a singular brush that glosses over the strikingly diverse and widely heterogeneous components that went into the formation of the Roman soul.[28] Underlying this seemingly homogeneous outer shell there are to be found many underground veins flowing into the Roman stock that were in continuous struggle with one another and bifurcated into TWO SOULS, better known by their social

---

[27] Archaic Rome – Refers to ancient Roman society of the pre-Republican reign of twelve Roman kings. The King of Rome (Latin: Rex Romae) was the chief magistrate of the Roman Kingdom. According to legend, the first king of Rome was Romulus, who founded the city in 753 BC upon the Palatine Hill. Seven legendary kings are said to have ruled Rome until 509 BC, when the last king, Lucius Tarquinius Superbus was overthrown. The kings after Romulus were not known to be dynasts and no reference is made to the hereditary principle until after the fifth king Tarquinius Priscus. Consequently, some have assumed that the Tarquins and their attempt to institute a hereditary monarchy over the earlier elective monarchy resulted in the formation of the Republic.

[28] Roman Soul – Julius Evola, *La Tradizione di Roma*, Edizioni di Ar, 1977. Julius Evola, *Revolt Against the Modern World*, Inner Traditions International, 1995. J.J. Bachofen, *Myth, Religion and Mother Right*, Princeton University Press, 1967.

classifications as patrician and plebeian[29] orders. These twin souls are best referred to by the names attributed to the founders of Rome, the Romulean soul and the Remean soul.

We find these two irrevocably divergent souls present from the founding and throughout the course of Roman history or *romanitas*[30] to modern Italian times. The clash of these competing and contrasting souls or spiritual orientations came to a head during the three Punic wars pitting Carthage against Rome. It was at the height of these conflicts when the Carthaginian armies of Hannibal (218-202 BC) were ravaging Italy, that communities across the Italian peninsula were forced to choose either between lending their support behind an autochthonous Hesperiam or invading Austral side. The soul of the future Italic peoples was at stake. Overwhelmingly, most of the communities sided with Rome, however, some

---

[29] Patricians and Plebeians – According to Livy, the first 100 men appointed as senators by Romulus were referred to as "fathers" (Latin: *patres*), and the descendants of those men became the patrician class. According to other opinions, the patricians (*patricii*) were those who could point to fathers, i.e. those who were members of the clans (*gentes*). The patricians were distinct from the plebeians because they had wider political influence, at least in the times of the early Republic. As the middle and late Republic saw this influence stripped, plebeians were granted equal rights in a range of areas, and quotas of officials, including one of the two consulships, were exclusively reserved for plebeians. At the beginning of the Republic, patricians were better represented in the Roman assemblies, only patricians could hold political offices, and all priesthoods were closed to non-patricians. There was a belief that patricians communicated better with the Roman gods, so they alone could perform the sacred rites and take the auspices.

[30] Romanitas is a Latin word, first coined in the third century AD, meaning Roman-ness and has been used by modern historians as shorthand to refer to Roman identity and self-image. Romanitas is the broader term for the political, cultural, religious, and social customs by which the Romans defined themselves.

tribes went over and allied themselves with Carthage. The
final victory of Rome over Carthage resulted in Italy and,
by extension, the western world (Hesperia), remaining
within a Septentrional and Occidental tradition associated
with the legendary Hyperborean and Atlantean traditions
that are distinct from the Austral and Oriental traditions.

Bachofen on Olympic Virility

One of the first authors to develop a deeper and more
compelling narrative of the internal components that went
into the formation of ancient Roman society is the Swiss
historian Johann Jacob Bachofen.[31] Bachofen developed

---

[31] Johann Jakob Bachofen (1815–1887) was a Swiss antiquarian,
jurist, philologist, anthropologist, and professor for Roman law at the
University of Basel from 1841 to 1845. Bachofen is most often connected
with his theories surrounding prehistoric matriarchy and his seminal
book *Das Mutterrecht* (*Mother Right: An Investigation of the Religious
and Juridical Character of Matriarchy in the Ancient World, 1861*).
Bachofen assembled documentation demonstrating that motherhood
is the source of human society, religion, morality, and decorum. He
postulated an archaic "mother-right" within the context of a primeval
Matriarchal religion or Urreligion. In his work on the ancient
Mediterranean mother right, *Das Mutterrecht*, Bachofen proposed four
phases of cultural evolution which absorbed each other:

1. Hetaerism: A wild nomadic 'tellurian' [chthonic or earth-centered] phase, characterized as communistic and polyamorous, whose dominant deity he believed to have been an earthy proto Aphrodite.

2. Lunar: A matriarchal 'lunar' phase based on agriculture, characterized by the emergence of chthonic mystery cults and law. Its dominant deity was an early Demeter.

3. Dionysian: A transitional phase when earlier traditions were masculinized as patriarchy began to emerge. Its dominant deity was the original Dionysus.

4. Apollonian: The patriarchal 'solar' phase, in which all trace of the Matriarchal and Dionysian past was eradicated and modern

a grand overview of the universal stages of the ancient world that is best summarized as a clash between societies oriented towards an uranian or spiritual "Father-Right" and those that were oriented more towards an earth-bound, corporal, and materialistic "Mother-Right."

Bachofen's own preoccupation with the universality and inescapability of this confrontation of societies between the feminine-material and the masculine-spiritual principles was the leitmotif or pre-eminent force that empowered Rome to assume a dominant world-historical role, and anticipated the struggle within the ancient world's most resplendent phenomenon: Rome and its empire.

The dual aspect of the city on the Tiber to the Orient, was described by Bachofen "... on the one side its dependence on it and on the other the external and internal overcoming of the Asiatic idea of the world and humanity," which can be seen in the Tanaquil myth.[32] In *Die Sage van Tanaquil*, a rich and authoritative allegorical account of the relationship between Roman and ancient oriental kingship published in 1870, Bachofen develops an evolutionary framework for the distinct femininities within the narrative of the world-historical role of Rome. Rome carried out the task which Greece had begun but was too weak to complete, of overcoming the matriarchal East and asserting a patriarchal civilization against it. Roman civilization purifies itself by defeating the Orient within Italy, hence the subtitle of the work:

---

civilization emerged.

[32] Tanaquil Myth – Tanaquil was the Etruscan wife of the Roman king of Etruscan descent, Tarquinius. Bachofen repeatedly uses the term Knechtschaft or "serfdom" to describe the condition of the male participant in this kingship of the Orient. At the heart of that realm was a priestly or "theocratic" kingship where power had a feminine legitimation. Tanaquil is the figure associated with this ancient tradition.

An Investigation of Orientalism in Rome and Italy. In the course of the struggle, political authority was torn away from a "theocratic" feminine power and came to rest on the Roman state. The ancient oriental kings had derived their authority from feminine figures, whose religious significance was inseparable from their sexual exuberance: the East represented a corporeal religiosity and a femininity tied to it; the patriarchal West a spiritual and incorporeal one. Having investigated this Oriental prehistory of Italy, Bachofen titled the last section of the work "the Roman transformation of the Asiatic heritage." "If we have seen that the Italic people took up Oriental ideas and customs to the fullest extent, so we will now see," he wrote in his introductory outline, "that the power of transformation of all those alien elements, and their subjection under its own form of thought, fully corresponds to its receptive power."

For Bachofen, the movement from passivity into willed assertiveness is at the same time distant from the theocratic foundation of the East. What Bachofen had regarded as Rome's original strength in his history of 1850, the ubiquity of "superstition", the fear and seeking of the *augurium*, was now, in 1870, a quality transferred by him to the feminine East: "If according to the same principle of passivity the Asiatic interpretation of any, even the most meaningless phenomenon, is a demoralized one and all strength of the spirit is abjectly wasted in anxious trepidation before the least of natural events, the Roman preserves the superiority of human understanding by means of the right to dismiss any augurium."

It is here that his entire conception of Rome's assimilation and transformation of eastern tradition, its move away from the "theocratic" eastern kingship, its "national" self-conception and world-historical role, and its separateness from and superiority to Greece, was articulated most convincingly. It's clear that Bachofen regards this episode as the most illustrative of the relationship between the feminine East and the Roman-led West. This mentality and this development concerned the progression from Asiatic passivity to western movement. The energy and severity of Rome, derived from its struggle with the Orient, had made possible the "historical" as opposed to "natural" existence of the West. We have seen that Bachofen regarded Rome as possessed of "ethical strength". The struggle which has become the hallmark of Europeans "becomes dominant in Rome", insisting on the "ethical strength" of Rome and its primacy as the most energetic political force in the ancient world compared to the sensualism and abortive heroism of Greece.[33]

Bachofen's theories on ancient Mediterranean culture had a profound influence on the twentieth century Italian philosopher of Traditional studies, Julius Evola. Bachofen's considerable influence can be found in Evola's writings on the Roman tradition and especially in his principal work on the metaphysics of history – *Revolt Against the Modern World*. Following in Bachofen's wake, Evola proposes the theory of two opposing spiritual poles, reflected in the patricians vs. plebeians, that parallel Bachofen's: Uranian and Tellurian currents feeding the ancient Roman souls. According to Evola, it was the contrasting spiritual differences that separated the patricians from plebeians in terms of religious practices and funerary rites that took precedence of importance over commercial or domestic differences which represent bourgeois tendencies. In Evola's exposition, the exclusivity of the patricians to hold religious rites and celebrate the Olympian cults along with the widespread practice among patricians to perform

---

[33] Damian Valdez, Bachofen's Rome and the Fate of the Feminine Orient, *Journal of the History of Ideas*, v.70, pp.421-443.

incinerary rites for their dead, in common with Vedic practices of the time, contrasted with plebeian customs that were inclined more to inhume their dead; which in the final analysis, were signs of uranian/cosmic vs. tellurian/chthonian spiritual differences. From the schema derived by this analysis, we can see a Remean orientation or purview of values that embraced an antithetical southern polarity or matriarchal substratum, linked to the cult of nature, with a tendential earth-arrested or horizontal orientation of life, where the individual's destiny is closely tethered in communion to the telluric mother. This proclivity for chthonic and lunar types of consciousness is contrasted with the second type, which in historical terms is linked to the Indo-European tribes that migrated in the late Bronze Age, represented by a proto-Hyperborean typology that Evola refers to as Olympian because of their inherent Uranian or cosmic spirituality which is oriented vertically towards the summits of Mt. Olympus.[34]

The twin souls represent two fundamentally different polar archetypes underlying the course of the Italic (Roman and Italian) metamorphic trajectory. A Remean soul manifests from an horizontal leveling principle of metamorphosis from human to human, in contrast with

---

[34] Olympic – Julius Evola – *La Tradizione di Roma*, Edizioni di Ar, 1977. *Rassegna Italiana*, Fondazione Julius Evola, 2012, Razza e Cultura p.65. "When a being owes to the forces of instinct and blood all that gives form and support to his life, he still belongs to nature. In the case of a human being, on this basis it can also develop superior qualities, but natural qualities will always remain an expression of nature. Here we find a style which, if it takes as its raw material and vehicle, "nature" does not allow itself to be reduced to the presence and action of a metabolic element of order."

J.J. Bachofen, *Le Madri e la Virilità Olimpica: Storia segreta dell'antico mondo mediterraneo*, Edizioni Mediterraneo, 2013.

Julius Evola, *Meditations on the Peaks: Mountain Climbing as a Metaphor for the Spiritual Quest*, Inner Traditions, 1998.

a Romulean soul whose metamorphic manifestation jettisons towards a vertical trajectory of transcendence, from human to the divine via the heroic spirit.

Heroic Spirit

Etymologically, the word *Hero* is closely related to Eros. Both derive from the same root, Amor (love), which corresponds to the hidden name of Rome (Roma, Amor, Maro, Orma).[35] In metaphysical terms, the *Urbs* (city, *polis*) represents the *Arcana mundi* (occult universe), the synthesis of feminine (venereal) and masculine (martial) vectors of forces. Although Rome is associated more with the chivalric nature of its martial form Mars (Maro), in spiritual terms the Arcana mundi of Rome is internally connected with Venus (Amor). Moreover, in ritual terms, Venerean initiation is propitious at certain cosmic junctions or transitional hours when Venus transits overhead, during the early morning prior to the appearance of dawn and late afternoon at the onset of dusk in the hour of Vespers (Greek ἑσπέρα for Hesperia). Amor is the "root principle" and "force in action" underlying the hero whether acting in the inner or outer planes. By embodying the principle of amor, the hero is set apart from the hubris of the Titans and usurpers of Tradition. The Hero grounded in a lineage linking ancestors with descendants, transcends the "*principium individuationis*" by rooting conscious identity to a spiritual ground, the Numen (soul). Viewed from an initiatic perspective, the Hero represents the transcended individual that has

---

[35] Hidden Name of Rome – Giandomencio Casalinio, *Il nome segreto di Roma: Metafisica della romanita*, Edizioni Mediterranee. Pietro De angelis, *Le origini di Roma e il suo nome segreto*, Arti Grafiche, Santa Barbara.

successfully journeyed through the underworld to arise on the other bank of the river Mnemosyne or Euone and finds his true sense of self, tradition, and homeland. By means of this katabasis, the human sheds the profane layers of his old self, in the initiatic death of his mundane (*humus*) nature and experiences *metanoia* or a complete ontological transfiguration into a new being of archetypal luminosity and vitality – the Hero.[36]

Atavistic Resurgence

Guarded within certain select, old, and well rooted Italic families, are claims concerning an uninterrupted lineage that can be traced back to distinguished ancestors of classical Rome. Likewise, zealously reserved within these same aristocratic circles, is the practice of arcane family rites that pertain to atavistic operations connecting descendants with the spirits (*umbra*) of illustrious forebears. Initiates are found among long standing clans (*gens*): Iulii, Claudii, Flavii, Symmachii, and later within medieval Roman families such as Colonnas, Massimos, and Caetani, to name a few. It was a mark of distinction among the Gens Julia to vaunt their family origins,

---

[36] Age of Heroes – After the bronze age Zeus created another race, an honorable race of heroes, who were noble and respected the gods. Among them were also individuals with divine qualities, called demi-gods. Most of them died in wars such as the Trojan war and Seven against Thebes. The souls of those, who passed away, went to a special place called the Elysian Fields or the Islands of the Blessed, in the underworld, surrounded by deep-swirling Oceanus. It was a place where the souls would remain forever and live a happy life in the same role they had enjoyed in life. It is also said that Zeus eventually promoted his father Cronus, from the depths of Tartarus, to become a ruler of the souls of these righteous and significant people. Men were now closer to animals, both eating meat but without fire. Man's position is faraway from the god's that he emulated.

stemming from the goddess Venus, through Aeneas, the progenitor of the Romans, and through the first king, Romulus, founder of the city. It is said that during funeral orations, Julius Caesar would recall ancestral families to remind his fellow Patricians of their own divine descent. In ancient Roman society, the sacerdotal priests, Flamines, were responsible for upholding the *mores maiorum*—mores of the ancestors—within society. The public mores constituted a veritable rule of force, the civic glue that ensures a healthy and virtuous populace remain attached to their roots. The mores maiorum were cited as codes of conduct to ennoble the present by recalling the past, and as a benchmark of *dignitas* by which Romans could reference their deeds.

The metaphor of trees is frequently referenced throughout Roman history to account for the health of society. Their comparatively human lifespan is a fitting metaphor for the beginning and ending of dynasties and for the vitality, triumph, and decline of select lineages. For example, the trees planted by Augustus' wife, Livia were reputed to have lasted for the duration of the Julio-Claudian dynasty. Romulus' fig tree, mentioned by Tacitus, perversely declined and withered to extinction at the onset of Nero's reign. These types of associations correlate in a consistent manner with the rise and fall of dynasties and political systems via the flourishing or withering of auspicious trees. The ancient Romans maintained long-standing family "trees" that metaphorically reference the genealogical "branches" (*rami*), "stock" (stirpes), and "sap" (royal/heroic bloodlines, *sanguis*) among old patrician families. Many of the attributes associated with leading Roman families are drawn from the planting, adoption, and uprooting of trees and their vitality is often described in human metaphors. Historians like Columella and Pliny use metaphors of abandonment, uprootedness, and adultery of agriculture and horticulture for the estrangement of dynasties from ancient traditions.[37]

In the parlance of ancient sacerdotal castes, mythologies play out as divine forms unbridled by earthly constraints that are fueled by cosmic forces, undulating within inner space and transmitted by seers in the form of visions or—in traditional terms—augurs and divinations. The human mind that receives spiritual influences from the font of archetypal forces in the form of inspirations, insights, or foresights is the divine mind.

The Golden Bough myth references a consistent language of signifiers and markers that manifest throughout the history of Roman and Italian eras. The appearance of auspicious origins, Renaissances, Rebirths, Risorgimentos, Renovatios, and Resurgences bear witness to the cyclical renewal of this form of atavistic resurgence. The symbolic codes grafted onto the principal parameters employed by Virgil in his role as Vates (seer) to articulate the inner language of the Golden Bough initiation, are decoded in the following terms:

- Golden Bough – votive branch to activate atavistic channels with spiritual ancestors, tutelary spirits and archetypes, Air or Vital Element
- Portal – initiation, magical door, transposition from the profane to the sacred
- Sacred grove – sacred realm of the tribe, Hesperia
- Underworld – astral world, inner realm, Invisible Empire
- Venus – Amor, uranian, divine or sacred love, universal energetic field, tutelary spiritual force, water element

---

[37] Emily Gowers, Trees and Family Trees in the *Aeneid*, *Classical Antiquity*, Vol.30, No.1.

- Persephone – Terrestrial love (eros), guardian of the threshold to the underworld, earth element
- Diana – Maternal love, divine matrix, lunar nature
- Two Doves – Dual nature, solar and lunar aspects of the purified initiate, Hero
- Oracle Sibyl – Vates, seer, diviner, poet, philosopher, custodian of tradition, journey guide, miner of roots, i.e. Virgil, Dante, Bruno, Kremmerz, Evola
- Anchises – Atavistic node of the Dardanian blood lines[38]
- Aeneas – Self, Archetype, Hero, seeker, initiate, artifex – Orpheus, Pythagoras, Hermes

---

[38] Dardanian Lineage – According to ancient legends, Aeneas was the son of Anchises the King of Dardania, and Aphrodite. He was the cousin of Hector and Paris, and also their brother-in-law. He was married to Creusa, daughter of Priam of Troy (the father of Hector and Paris). Aeneas led the Dardanians against the invading Greeks during the Trojan War. After the sack of Troy, he escaped with his father Anchises, son, and wife. He and his followers eventually settled in Italy, founding Alba Longa and eventually Rome. Dardanus is the son of Jupiter and of the Pleiade Electra. He was born in Corito, near the Etruscan city of Tarquinia. Anchises was a member of the royal family of Troy in Greek and Roman legends. Homer, in the *Iliad*, and later Virgil, reminds us that Aeneas belongs to the lineage of Dardanus, just as the royal family of Priam does. The history of Dardanus' journey should not, however, be relegated to being a simple myth. It is perfectly reflected in an ancient custom attributed to the first Indo-European migrations. Under the light of Mars, entire groups of young warriors were forced to leave the tribe of origin to discover and eventually colonize new fertile or uninhabited territories.

Italic Tree of Life

The Golden Bough is a votive branch used in archaic initiation rituals to attain gnosis with the radix of the tradition.

In the Virgilian myth, the Golden Bough functions as a conductor in initiatory operations to connect the initiate with the *radix* (roots) of his lineage and receive spiritual influences (presence, inspirations, intuitions, guidance, virtues, auspicious messaging) from the archetypes of the tribe – ancestors, kings, heroes, and gods. The Golden Bough is a consecrated instrument that has been ritually charged and coded with signifiers sacred to the tribe and is immediately felt as a symbolic manifestation of invisible forces. The initiation establishes a branch or process of conductivity through which the ancestral spirit (sap) flows through subtle channels from the archetypal roots of the tribe to the initiate. The Rex, in his dual role of Warrior and Sacerdot, is the solar initiator, the lord of the rite and *artifex* of the ascetic sacrifice by which men are "transfigured and transformed" into initiates along the path. Forged by initiatory practice, men are transformed into *Vir* (an ancient Roman term for a nobleman in possession of innate virtue), which is a cognate for the Vedic term *Virya* (hero), and with the ancient Runic sigil for fire – VR. This network of symbols is related to the element of fire, located at the spiritual center – the heart reigns over the radiating power of love, light, and life. By connecting the dotted lines of the constituent pieces that make up this Arcana, we are led to acknowledge a fundamental metaphysical truth that underlies and equates the Roman Vir (hero) with the synthesis of Venerean (amor) and Martial (will) forces. The Roman Vir is characterized by the integration and synthesis of Solar and Lunar or Martial and Venerean principles. The

Golden Bough serves as a metaphor for the Tree of Life by means of its capacity to transmit the sacred fire (integrated consciousness-life force) of the tribe from one generation to the next.

We shall cite throughout this study examples of guides, seers, visionaries, poets, philosophers and the tools of their trade: symbols, myths, sigils, archaeological remnants, doves, woods of life, etc. that serve the same purpose of re-awakening spiritual archetypes for the tribe, by inspiring seekers to reclaim an identity and, also at the risk of tempting fate, attempting another restoration of the Hesperian (Olympian) tradition and Ghibelline empire.

Ars Italica

This study seeks to survey a broad spectrum of inner traditions and bring to light, the heroes, schools, and teachings that have laid the groundwork for initiation in Italy, from Roman times to the present, and in the broader sense of an Occidental tradition. The underlying themes that inform this initiation include: a perennial Western Empire (Hesperia), Atavistic Resurgences and internal practices specific to the *Italic Ars*: *heroica, magia, amatoria, memoria, imaginatio, insomnium,* and *metamorphosis*. Initiation in this context, from the Latin *initiātus*, refers to the individual inner journey to identify and integrate with the Principle (Self, Soul, Numen) and the Tradition (Olympian, Heroi, Aeneadean) associated with that principle. In this sense, initiation, like Aeneas' quest to divine the future by finding the roots of his past (principle) refers to a process of self-discovery by exercising deep-levels of consciousness – the constant interaction between the imaginatio (imagination), somnium (dreams), and memoria (memory) to create a living identity through the exercise of recollection, connectivity, intuition, and creation. The operation of re-integrating with the principle of the Self occurs as a result of reversing the polarity of the initiate's center of being from external and exogenous influences to a center that is nourished internally from spiritual roots (Numen). The spiritually integrated initiate is ontologically transformed and perfected into an adept (hero) that embodies the perfect synthesis of the Solar (male) and Lunar (female) principles. The perfect union of these sidereal principles is sealed when the outer transformation integrates with the inner and the initiate undergoes a metamorphosis into an Artifex, or *Homo Faber*. In the words of the sapient Giambattista Vico – "*Verum esse ipsum factum*" (Truth is that which is made). He who creates makes truth. The hero in his capacity as truth maker, wields the tools of his trade—myths, symbols, rituals, dreams, and ideas—to create new forms of truth that shape reality.

This study makes no claims to speak the final word, rather with modest intentions, the emphasis is more on clarity of exposition than depth of explanation, and in the words of a contemporary practitioner of initiation, Giammaria, serves no more than to leave a trace for a future memory to return and elaborate further on this tradition.[39]

The criteria for determining what and who to include in the following pages, are summarized as follows:

- Scope: Western, Classical and Italic inner traditions
- Subjects: Heroes, initiates, poets, philosophers, visionaries

---

[39] Giammaria, Preface to *Conversations on Hermeticism* (*Dissertamina*) by Marco Daffi, Edizioni Alkaest.

- Vehicles: initiatory orders, schools based in Italy or in the Roman Empire
- Material: philosophies, initiation, wisdom, esoterica, testimonies, poetries
- Value: foundational, innovators, impact, influences

ORIGINS

Return of the Nostoi (Olympians)[40]

In the long history of the many diverse peoples occupying the peninsula that branches out from the southern flank of Europe, now known as Italy and previously as Hesperia, Ausonia, Enotria, and Saturnia. The presence of traditions (cults, sodalities, schools) dedicated to the spiritual elevation of consciousness dates back to the dawn of Western civilization. Seen from a Traditional perspective, the wheel of time is understood as a continuous cycle of eras, or what the ancient Indo-Āryas of the Vedic tradition refer to as *Yugas*. Ancient mythologies reference the existence of a Golden Age in archaic Italy, known as Saturnia Tellus,[41] under the reign

---

[40] Olympians are a race of seekers that undertook heroic feats referred to as quests or missions to attain a level of freedom and powers over the human condition. They are characterized by a quest, seeking to exceed beyond the mundane nature of ordinary humans. Olympians are set apart from ordinary mortals by their pursuit of the vertical tangent. An internal conquest, requisition, and affirmation of divine virtues over external forces within the laws of the cosmos. Examples: Thetis, Jason, Aeneas, Romulus.

[41] Saturnia Tellus - "*Salve magna Parens frugum, Saturnia tellus, Magna Virum*" ("Hail the Land of Saturn, great parent of fruits and men" (Virgil, *Georgiche*, II, 173).

of primitive divinities headed by Saturn (*Sat*: Being, *Urn*: Era). This Golden Age was followed by a Silver Age – ruled by Jupiter and the Olympians, and characterized by the preponderance of mystery cults associated with cosmic powers that synthesized the sidereal forces of Jupiter, Apollo, Mars, Venus, etc. and the telluric forces of birth, death, and renewal as found in the cults of Dionysus, Demeter, and Ceres. This cycle was followed by a Bronze Age that was interrupted before the advent of the Iron era, with the restoration of a new order led by heroes with royal lineages linked to upholding values of the Olympians. The heroic age bequeathed future generations with the foundational components of Western civilization that included archetypes and traditions rooted in a way of life that henceforth has been referred to as the Royal Path. The end of the heroic age corresponded with the end of the archaic epoch and precipitated the beginning of the Iron era or historical age, characterized by the reign of toil, dissolution, and materialism.

Schola Italica - Pythagorean School of Italy

The founding of an Italic School of initiatic teachings based in Croton, Calabria was established by the philosopher, ascetic, and initiate Pythagoras (530 BC). This marked an important milestone in the diffusion of a

---

The expression Saturnia Tellus (Earth of Saturn) in the Roman religion indicates the kingdom of the god Saturn during the mythical land of the Golden Age, initiated after expulsion from Olympus. The god was first ousted by his son Jupiter and exiled to Italy, where he found refuge in Lazio and placed his kingdom there. The land of Saturn was first identified in Lazio and then, more generally, with Italy where Saturn was considered the first king. The Latin poets and Virgil in particular, celebrated Italy as Saturnia Tellus. *Bucolic,* Fourth Eclogue on the Golden Age, The Greetings of Virgil to Italy.

distinct Occidental vector of initiation that differed from prevailing Near Eastern and Asian forms. The Pythagorean school was organized into sodalities (fraternal orders) that were laboratories of experimentation and fundamental to the development of spiritual sciences, associated with the purification, recollection, and transmigration of consciousness. Later in the same century, the Greek philosopher Parmenides set roots in (Elea) Southern Italy and founded a school known as the Eleatics whose search for truth was based on the principle of *Aletheia*, on the premise that reality, at its essence, is reduced to an unchanging, ungenerated, and indestructible source of Being.

From the 5th century BC onward, various schools of initiation were established throughout Magna Graecia (Southern Italy) and were for the most part extensions of the numerous philosophical schools that flourished throughout the passage from the Roman Republic to the Empire.

The Underground Pythagorean Basilica of Porta Maggiore[42]

In the late Republic, the Roman senator Publius Nigidius Figulus (98–45 BC) was a leading figure of Roman gentility. He was an erudite man renowned for his vast wisdom, rectitude of character, and powerful

---

[42] Underground Basilica of Porta Maggiore – Hans van Kasteel, *La Basilique secrète de la Porte Majeure ou Le Temple de Virgile,* Beya, 2016. Nuccio D'Anna, *Nigidio Figulo. Un pitagorico a Roma nel 1 secolo a.c.*, Editore Pizeta. Jerome Carcopino, *La basilique pythagoricienne de la Porte Majeure*, Paris, l'Artisan du livre, 1927.

Alberto Gianola, *Publio Nigidio Figulo Astrologo e Mago*, Biblioteca Teosofica.

oratory skills. Figulus also had a predication for occult practices that led to founding a sodality to implement Pythagorean and other esoteric practices in Rome. The sodality consisted of practitioners who converged in a subterranean basilica, located near the Porta Maggiore on the Via Praenestina in central Rome, to practice what are understood to be initiatic rituals that most likely involved the exercise of magical and theurgical practices. The sodality was influential in reviving esoteric teachings that counter balanced the more exoteric methods espoused by the dominant philosophies of Epicureanism and Stoicism.

On the 21st of April, 1917, excavations to the embankment of the Rome-Naples railway gave way a short distance outside the Porta Maggiore: repair of the damage led to the discovery of a subterranean building believed to be a Basilica from the Classical period of ancient Rome. One may say, without fear of exaggeration, that this is one of the most important discoveries ever made in Rome, and it raises a formidable number of archaeological, historical, and artistic problems.

Walls and vaulting of both the Basilica and *atrium* are covered with magnificent stucco reliefs, pure white in the Basilica itself and brilliantly colored in the atrium where the light must have been very much greater. The building at the Porta Maggiore[43] shows that pagan halls were also preceded by *atria*, and the remains of sacrifices found in the *impluvium* show that part of the ceremonies took place there, perhaps the sacrifice of initiation.

The greatest attraction of this extraordinary building consists in the stucco decoration of the interior. The common Roman decorative motives, candelabra, Gorgoneia, figures of Victories and of Orantes, sacred vessels and implements, alternate with scenes of Erotes

---

[43] Pythagorean Basilica at Porta Maggiore – Gilbert Bagnani, *The Journal of Roman Studies*, Vol. 9 (1919) pp.78-85.

and children's games, of sacrifices, tales of the pygmies, and with mythological subjects. The mythological representations are taken from the whole field of Graeco-Roman mythology. Especially notable are the representations of the rape of Helen, the freeing of Hesione, Jason seizing the fleece while Medea enchants the serpent, Heracles before one of the Hesperides, and the punishment of the daughter of Danaus. Some of the subjects are common enough while others are very rare, almost unique.

Another remarkable feature of the decoration is the presence, behind each of the pillars, of stucco portraits which are quite exceptional. Professor (Franz) Cumont suggests that they may be merely conventional representations of Greek sages, but, as they do not bear the slightest resemblance to any known portraits, I am inclined to consider them actual portraits of eminent members or benefactors of the sodalitas.

The chief value of the reliefs reside in the fact that they are our only clue to the purpose of the Basilica and to the religious beliefs of its founders. No trace can be found of any of the well-known Oriental cults such as the Kabeiroi, Kybele, Isis, or Mithras, while the Dionysian scenes are merely decorative in character. What is perfectly clear is that the builders believed in the immortality of the soul. The Victories that form such a large part of the decoration undoubtedly allude to the triumph over death. In the *apse*, just above the throne, a Nike stands between two worshipers, to one of whom she is holding out a wreath, the symbol of immortality. The frequently repeated scenes of the rape of Leucippides and that of the liberation of Hesione, symbolize the rape of the soul by the powers of death and its liberation from earthly chains. The striking analogy that this relief has with the numerous representations of the Imperial Apotheosis renders it probable that the artist's intention was to depict the Apotheosis of the soul.

On the right a heavily-veiled woman with a seven-stringed lyre in her hand is being pushed off a rock by an Eros who stands behind her. It has been suggested that the artist meant to represent Sappho's leap from the Leucadian rock and that he was directly influenced by Ovid's famous epistle (Heroidum epistulae, xv,157-184).

Professor Cumont considers the Basilica to have been the meeting-place of one of those Neo-Pythagorean sects whose greatest Roman representative was Nigidius Figulus. The scene in the apse represents the journey of the soul to the islands of the Blessed, which in Neo-Pythagorean philosophy represents the Sun and the Moon, islands in the sea of Aether, and therefore, on one of them stands Apollo the Sun-God. The woman personifies the Soul impelled towards the stars by celestial love, and the seven stringed lyre in her hand symbolizes the celestial harmony.

Cicero and the Art of Dreaming

Marcus Tullius Cicero's (106-43 BC) classic work on dream work, the appropriately titled *Somnium Scipionis* (*The Dream of Scipio*) had a profound and long-lasting effect on the literary and philosophical milieus of classical Rome. Acknowledged as Rome's leading statesman, lawyer, consul, orator and writer, Cicero's *Somnium* was the concluding section of his book on good government, *De Re Publica*. In the *Somnium* Scipionis elaborates on the nature of the Soul, on divine and heroic virtues, from a Stoic perspective. The story takes place in a dream and narrates the journey of Scipio's "disembodied soul", giving rise to the possibility of astral projections and oneiric journeys. The work draws upon practices taught in the ancient mystery schools, including the hermeneutics on various dream types and their augural significance.

THE VATIC POETS

Virgil and Ovid are widely acknowledged as the two poets having the greatest impact on Latin literature. Although better known for having written literary classics, their body of work covers a broad range of esoteric teachings on initiation and self-transformation that are fundamental to the Western inner traditions.

Virgil[44]

There is an art that allows us to attain in life what the power of souls of the dead have realized beyond the threshold of death,

---

[44] Virgil – The *Aeneid* has been considered the national epic of ancient Rome since the time of its composition. Modeled after Homer's *Iliad* and *Odyssey*, the *Aeneid* follows the Trojan refugee Aeneas as he struggles to fulfill his destiny and reach Italy, where his descendants Romulus and Remus were to found the city of Rome. Tradition holds that Virgil was born in the village of Andes, near Mantua in Cisalpine Gaul (added to Italy during his lifetime). Analysis of his name has led to beliefs that he descended from earlier Roman colonists. Modern speculation ultimately is not supported by narrative evidence either from his own writings or his later biographers. Relatively little is known about the family of Virgil. His father reportedly belonged to gens Vergilia, and his mother belonged to gens Magia.

Why, when life leaves them at the final hour,

still all of the evil, all the plagues of the flesh, alas,

have not completely vanished, and many things, long hardened

deep within, must of necessity be ingrained, in strange ways.

So they are scourged by torments, and pay the price

for former sins: some are hung, stretched out,

to the hollow winds, the taint of wickedness is cleansed

for others in vast gulfs, or burned away with fire:

each spirit suffers its own: then we are sent

through wide Elysium, and we few stay in the Elysium fields,

for lengths of days, till the cycle of time

complete, removes the hardened stain, and leaves

pure ethereal thought, and the brightness of natural air.

All these others the god calls in a great crowd to the river Lethe,

after they have turned the wheel for a thousand years,

so that, truly forgetting, they can revisit the vault above,

and begin with a desire to return to the flesh.

-Virgil, *Aeneid*, VI, Transmigration of the Soul

Virgil (Publius Vergilius Maro, 70-19 BC), was born near Mantua in Cisalpine Gaul[45] (Northern Italy) and wrote

---

[45] Cisalpine Gaul - Also called Gallia Cisalpina, Gallia Citerior ("Near Gaul"), Provincia Ariminum, or Gallia Togata ("Toga-wearing Gaul", indicating the region's early Romanization). Gallia Transpadana denoted that part of Cisalpine Gaul between the Padus (now the Po River) and the Alps, while Gallia Cispadana was the part to the south of

three major works – *Aeneid*, *Bucolics*, and the *Georgics*. Over the course of his highly lauded vocation as Rome's pre-eminent poet, Virgil's work came to epitomize Romanitas (Romanness) in style and content. As a young man he attended the Epicurean school of Naples under the tutelage of the philosopher Siro. The bay of Naples at the time was a burgeoning center of esoteric learning with many philosophical schools, such as those of Platonic, Neo-Pythagorian, Epicurean, and Stoic provenance. Naples was also an epicenter for the many Mediterranean mystery cults that flourished in the first centuries of the Empire. A fresco painted on the wall of a Villa near Pompeii, known to the public as the Villa of Mysteries, was excavated last century after remaining buried since the eruption of Mt. Vesuvius in 79 AD. The fresco depicts a Roman woman taking part in a Bacchic initiation. Similarly, in book six of the *Aeneid*, Virgil narrates an Orphic initiation or katabasis that involves the aspirant taking part in a spiritual descent through the underworld to attain a purification of consciousness and resurgence of the soul that transforms the individual into an Hero.

The influence Virgil yielded as a Vates with divine insight was established early on in his vocation as poet and writer. He inspired legends associated with magic, prophecy, and even transgressing death. His name was conjured in magical operations and his writings referenced for mantic prognosis. Legends concerning Virgil and his innate magical powers retained value from imperial Roman times, throughout the middle ages and up to the Renaissance. Already by the third century, Christian scholars began to interpret Eclogues four of the *Bucolics*, known as the "Messianic Eclogue", as the revelation of a new Golden Age in connection with the birth of a

---

the river. Virgil, Catullus, and Livy, three famous sons of the province, were born in Gallia Cisalpina.

figure 4 – Virgil

messianic child. As a result, Virgil became associated with prophetic powers and as a Vates who predicted the Messiah's birth and heralded Christianity.

The *Bucolics* and the *Georgics* portray a new Golden Age through the panorama of a return to a rural paradise, which was referred to by the ancient elegiac poets such as Theocritus, as Arcadia. This vision of a renewed Golden Age was characterized as a more virtuous and nobler society, cleansed from the corruption and strife of urban Rome, and as an universal age of pacification separate from the bloodshed on the battlefields around the Empire. Virgil depicts this Golden Age in terms of a return to the abandoned countryside, to toil on the farm, till the soil, cultivate the vine, and practice the natural religiosity of cosmos, hearth, and spirit. Through the exercise of vatic powers, Virgil's epic tales cast myths in a sublime form that seed the consciousness of the individual and the collective mind with aspirations, ideals, and visions of what the Western world could become. The myths took root among some of the more dissimilar elements of society, such as cultured citizens and legionnaires returning from battle who aspired to live the rest of their lives in peace and harmony with the natural order.

Magical Realism in the Roman Empire

Magical realism is an approach to life that weaves the surreal into everyday existence to provide a more thorough experience and understanding of life's great procession. Moreover, the poet who knows how to shape the minds of individuals and the collective community at large through the application of inspired imagination—imagery, mythology, and phantasmagoria—is also a magus.

What is real and what is imaginary? In the world of magical realism, the ordinary becomes extraordinary and the magical becomes commonplace.

There are four major themes to Virgil's magical realism:

1. Aeneas – Roman occidental archetype representing collective duty and individual transcendence
2. Heroic initiation – Golden Bough katabasis
3. Return to the land – Blood, soil, and spirit
4. Return of a Golden Age – *Aureum Saeculum Nova* – Hesperia

Typically, within ordinary states of consciousness, perception occurs as a function within a physical frame of reference and therefore events that take place in an existential setting simultaneously permeate multiple levels of consciousness—surface, subconscious, and unconscious—and can arise as a residual manifestation within a dream or as a subconscious fear. The same impact or influence can occur in reverse, whereby the initiate operating in the astral plane affirms himself as a conscious protagonist in dream scenarios that can influence the character of waking consciousness in a physical environment.

In a state of ecstatic inspiration the poet can change his frame of reference at will by re-configuring the mind from within the body to the body within the mind. In this alternate state of consciousness, the poet/magus has greater freedom and plasticity with the tools of his craft to exercise his magical imagination through visions to articulate images and thought forms that pervade the inner world and shape everyday existential reality.

As a result of wielding his formidable powers as poet, Vates, magus, and dreamweaver of Imperial Rome, Virgil was able to conjure a potent vision that was deeply embedded in the archetypal foundation of Western man. This inspiration or projection of conscious energy through the vehicles of imagery and mythos articulated in his works provided a collective vision for a future Western world based on the synthesis of venerean and martial principles and manifested as love, work, and peace. This ideal of a future Western world constituted as an harmonious order is known as the PAX ROMANA.

Ovid

Fortune and love favor the bold. – Audentum, Forsque, *Venusque juvant*, Ars Amatoria, Book 1[46]

The Classical Latin poet, Ovid (Publius Ovidius Naso, 43 BC–18 AD) wrote extensively on transformation (*Metamorphoses*) and Love (*Ars Amatoria & Amores*) from the heroic perspective of a protagonist in pursuit of the pursued. In the *Art of Love*, Ovid boldly advises inexperienced lovers to approach love with the same vigor, audacity, and cunningness as a soldier trained in war.

The art of *Metamorphosis* is the process of transformation, whether in ascent or descent, of the individual or collective. Ovid witnessed the turbulent transition of Rome from a republic (*res publica*) of the people controlled by a senate rooted in the patricians (nobles of indigenous tribes) to a cosmopolitan state headed by a dictator under the title of Caesar. The struggle between the two factions (Romulean/Republican

---

[46] Ovid, *Collected Works*, Loeb Classical library, 1989.

vs. Remean/Ceasaran) was a long and intense battle that touched on both gross and subtle levels. At stake was the fate of Italy's destiny. The political metamorphosis from a Republic to an Empire resulted in a polar shift of paradigms from a predominantly archaic tradition of Italy's indigenous people to a cosmopolitan-based dictatorship that was associated more with Oriental-Austral influences, and therefore, non-Roman. The republican partisans like Cato, Cicero, and Ovid were harsh critics of the embryonic development of a state dictatorship under the rule of a Ceasaran tyranny that was antithetical to the traditional Mos Maiorun and represented an oppositional Romanitas.

In contrast with Virgil, who extolled the Augustean rule as a new Golden Era, Ovid articulated an oppositional Romanitas. In fact, his opposition plays out in many ways as positive – a new Romanitas. Ovid challenged the ruling order in a subtle way. He countered the Augustean cult of patriarchy with the Heroides that exalted the feminine role in heroic culture. The Augustean promulgation of matrimony and monogamy was opposed by the heroic art of seduction—Ars Amatoria—and the rise of foreign cults was countered by extolling the ancient indigenous religious practices of the "*Fasti.*" His subversive actions did not go without notice and soon the celebrated poet was forced into exile to the far reaches of the empire on the northern shore of the Black Sea, home to the semi-civilized population (barbarians) of the Dacians. They are more than just great literary figures, Virgil and Ovid are referenced throughout the course of the Italic tradition (Romanitas) as Vates, oracles of spiritual truths and seers predicting the future form of Hesperia.

Apuleius and the Art of Metamorphoses

Apuleius of Madauros (124-174 AD) was recognized as an erudite author who wrote extensively on magic, myth, divination, and self-transformation. He wrote the classic tale of romance and transformation *The Golden Ass*. Apuleius' novel, also known as the *Metamorphoses,* contains hidden within its flowing narrative of wit and transgressions, a potent spiritual practice known as the "Contemplation of the Midnight Sun", that provides precious insights for the would-be initiate on how to harness self-will when transitioning between different states of consciousness. In the *Golden Ass*, the hero Lucio, is transformed into a donkey for having sought to practice the art of magic (without adequate knowledge) and he succumbs to lust and other worldly desires. Much of the novel takes place with Lucio embodied in the form of a donkey and revolves around his long search for a remedy to his affliction (asininity). After many attempts at repentance, purifications, and invocations to the holy goddess, Isis, the donkey (Lucio) receives liberation when he meets the priest of a mysterious sect who hands him a garland of roses. He eats these and immediately turns into a man, receiving initiation into the mysteries of Isis. Literally, this tale recounts the mystical drama in search of a rose (initiation), which refers to the mystical love of the nightingale (the soul) for the rose (initiation). The rose was an initiatory symbol, referenced in several traditions, including throughout the Renaissance as a special type of woman evoked by the Fedeli d'Amore (Faithful of love). It is also curious to note that the concept of asininity and its trope refers to a form of metamorphosis involving a descending transformation of man into beast that was taken up later in the Renaissance by Giordano Bruno.

Apuleius "The God of Socrates"[47]

> ... the human soul is a kind of daemon, that having finished its service in earthly life, retreats from the body: it is this soul that, in the ancient Latin language is also called "*lemur*".

Among these lemurs, therefore, the one who has the task of caring for his descendants and ruling the house with power (Numen), equable, and calm, is called *Lar familiaris*. Someone else, however, because of his misdeeds in earthly life, is deprived of his own seat and is condemned to wander aimlessly, as in an exile:

> ... vain and lost souls of man, a scourge for the wicked, this kind of daemon is a form of "*larvae*". In the event that it is uncertain which fate has affected them, whether a "*lar*" or a "*larva*", is also known as "*mani*": a daemon that is understood as an honorific title.

Paradoxically, it was at the height of the Roman Empire that an inversion of polarity took place with the weakening influence of italic traditions on the Roman state that resulted in the waning of indigenous tribal structures – families, lineages, and stirpes.[48] In contrast, the growing influence of foreign cults, especially those arriving from the Eastern provinces led to the flourishing of exotic teachings based on self purification, asceticism, and transcendence, especially within the academies and sodalities throughout the peninsula. Along this line of

---

[47] Apuleius – *The God of Socrates*, Thomas Taylor, Holmes Publishing Group, 2001.

[48] Italic component in the Roman legions dwindled to the point where by 100 AD there were more non-Italians in the military. At this point the Roman imperial army was composed mostly of mercenaries whose loyalties were questionable.

teaching, the Emperor Marcus Aurelius (121-161 AD) articulated a stoic-influenced practice designed to elevate individual consciousness away from the lower nature to higher levels of being and from the external to that which is internal. During the late Empire, Plotinus (204–270) and his disciple Porphyry (234–305) transmitted the Mediterranean mystery teachings on initiation through the exegesis of treatises on Neo-Pythagorean and Neo-Platonic philosophies. After which, the torch of tradition was passed over to the Syrian school led by the philosopher Iamblichus (245–325 AD) who promoted theurgy as the preferred means for the soul to ascend to divinity. Late into the Western Empire, Emperor Julian made worthy attempts through his philosophical works and political activities to reconstitute the ancient Roman traditions (Romanitas). The philosopher Sallust (Saturninius Secundus Salutius, 367 AD) was also part of a faction that promulgated the ancestral traditions of Rome and contributed the influential treatise *On the Gods and the Universe*. Sallust's work synthesizes Platonic and Pythagorean doctrines within the philosophical worldview laid out by the philosophies of the Emperor Julian. Sallust presents a vision of the world and of the sacred that falls within the context of the theurgical doctrines outlined by Iamblichus. He was a trusted advisor to Julian and accompanied the Emperor during his failed Parthian campaign where Julian was killed. Sallust was offered the purple upon Emperor Julian's death, however, he refused the investiture.[49]

---

[49] Sallust, *On the Gods and the World*, Createspace Independent Publishing Platform.

The Last of the Olympians – Symmachus & Macrobius

Late in the fourth century, Quintus Aurelius Symmachus (345–402 AD) belonged to one of the few remaining families that continued to practice Rome's ancient religious traditions. Quintus Aurelius Symmachus was a prominent Roman statesman, renowned for an earnest and simple style of oratory that secured for him a reputation as an influential orator and a man of letters. In 384 AD, he wrote to the new Emperor Valentinian II requesting the restoration of the "Altar of Victory", to celebrate and preserve Rome's ancient patrimony. The Altar of Victory was located in the Curia of the Roman Senate and bore a gold statue of the deity Victory to commemorate the victory of Augustus over Anthony and Cleopatra at the Battle of Actium.[50] One of the last sages to write on mystery traditions was Macrobius (430 AD), author of the *Saturnalia* and a *Commentary on the Dream of Scipio*, the classic work on ancestral dream initiation or *Ars Insomnium* by the Roman orator Cicero. Macrobius was heralded as an exceptional man by the city prefects and decreed with the honorary title Virs Inlustris.

MACROBIUS' COMMENTARY ON THE DREAM OF SCIPIO[51]

> We are also informed in words that cannot be mistaken that such divinity is present in the human race and that we are all ennobled by our kinship with the heavenly Mind…This is the condition that Plato

---

[50] 4L.M. Viola, Quinto Aurelio Simmaco, *Lo splendore della Romanitas*, Victrix.

Renato del Ponte, *In Difesa della Tradizione*, Relazione sulla rimozione del'ara della Vittoria, Arya.

[51] Macrobius, *Commentary on the Dream of Scipio*, Columbia University Press, pp.135-137.

called "at once indivisible and divisible" when he was speaking in the *Timaeus* about the construction of the World Soul. Souls, whether of the world or of the individual, will be found to be now unacquainted with division if they are reflecting on the singleness of their divine state... Now if souls were to bring with them to their bodies a memory of the divine order of which they were conscious in the heavens, there would be no disagreement among men in regard to their divinity; but indeed, all of them in their descent drink of forgetfulness, some more, some less... Be not disturbed that in reference to the soul, which we say is immortal, we so often use the term "death". In truth, the soul is not destroyed by death but is overwhelmed for a time, nor does it surrender the privilege of immortality because of its lowly sojourn, for when it has rid itself of all impurities and has deserved to be sublimated, it again leaves the body and, fully recovering its former state, returns to the splendor of everlasting life.

A fundamental precept of the Neo-Pythagorean and Neo-Platonic teachings is the Law of Emanation. This law refers to the hypostasisaic process of creation whereby the Supreme Source or Monad issues forth through the Cosmic Soul (Anima Mundi) to the individual soul (Numen). By virtue of its integration with the Monad, the hypostasis is spiritual in nature and separate from the material realm. The Pythagoreans and Platonists taught that the Dyad represents the non-spiritual (material) realm, the shadow of material change and corruption.

MACROBIUS ON THE NEO-PYTHAGOREAN LAW OF EMANATION[52]

In the first combination, the One is called monad, it is Unity, and is both male and female, odd and even, and is itself not a number, but the principle and source of numbers. The monad, is the beginning and ending of all things, yet itself doesn't know a beginning or ending. It refers to the supreme God, and separates our understanding of him (the One, without number) from the number of things and powers following: you would not be so rash as to look for it in a sphere lower than God. It is also that Mind, sprung from the Supreme God, which, unaware of the changes of time, is always in one time, the present; and although the monad is itself not numbered, it nevertheless produces from itself, and contains within itself, innumerable patterns of created things. Then, too, by giving a little thought to the matter, you will find that the monad refers to the Soul. Indeed, the Soul is free from contamination with anything material, owing only to its Creator and to itself, and being endowed with a single nature; that projects forth to animate the immense universe, it does not permit any division of its singleness. The monad, having sprung from the First Cause of things, is found everywhere undiminished and always indivisible, for it maintains the continuity of its powers even in regard to the Soul.

By the late 4th century, the families of Flavianus, Praetextatus and the previously mentioned Symmachus were the last bastions of clans (Gens) to uphold the ancient traditions, spiritual lineages, and blood lines passed down from the Olympian Age of Heroes.

> And if we believe that the underworld is in this body, what is to be understood by the death of the soul, if

---

[52] Macrobius, *On the Neopythagorean Law of Emanation*.

not its immersion in the underworld of the body and, for its life, its return to the supernal regions beyond, after it has left the body. – Macrobius, *Commentary on Scipio's Dream*, I, 10, 17

part
TWO

MIDDLE AGES/RENAISSANCE

Dante and the Fedeli d'Amore

Love that is stripped of banal sentimentalities and engaged as a naked force in magical evocation and transcendence, is in the words of the Divine poet "a love that moves the stars and suns".

After the turbulence that marked the centuries following the fall of the Roman Empire, with invasions and wars by foreign powers, the Italian Middle Ages was also characterized by a constant struggle for dominance between two warring factions that were either pro-Empire (Ghibelline) or pro-Papacy (Guelphs). After nearly a millennium of residing latent (Latium), we see emerge from the underground, rising like misty embers from under the Roman catacombs, the same two opposing forces, the twin Romulean and Remean souls that we've encountered previously, yet this time dressed in the clothes of Ghibellines and Guelphs.

In tangent with the jockeying of forces, the Italian soil was fertile with spiritual ferments. The most bountiful fruit was reaped by a circle of Poets who were seekers of the divine and known as the Fedeli d'Amore (Faithful of Love). Dante was the pre-eminent member of the circle and his epic poem the *Divine Comedy* is ripe with initiatic allegory. The Fedeli d'Amore practiced a mystical form of initiation where the force of love was heightened and distilled through a contemplative practice that utilized the magnetic power of the feminine compliment to raise consciousness upwards towards the divine. In Dante's ultra-mundane journey, depicted in the *Commedia,* the complex relationship between words and facts, between poetry and experience, pervades both the objective sphere of the narrative and the subjective dimension of the narration. On the one hand, the poet states his voyage was experienced in real terms, while on the other hand claiming the insufficiency of human language to articulate his extraordinary experience. In this perspective memory, imagination, and the ingenuity of expression play a fundamental role. The *Divine Comedy* could be read as a template for the alchemical opus: *Inferno* (*Nigredo*, black), *Purgatorio* (*Albedo*, white), and *Paradiso* (*Rubedo*, red). Seen from a traditional lens, the Fedeli d'Amore were the Faithful servants of Love, understood as the embodied vehicles of Amor, the divine power of love, which in the Dantean context represents the Ghibelline faction led by Federicus, Emperor of the Holy Roman Empire and known as the *"Stupor Mundi."*

The *trobar clus* of the *Divine Comedy* is resolved by discovering the occult affiliation linking Dante and the Fedeli d'Amore with Aeneas and the Aeneades.[53] The

---

[53] The Aeneades included Aeneas' trumpeter Misenus, his father Anchises, his friends Achates, Sergestus, and Acmon, the healer Lapyx, the steady helmsman Palinurus, and his son Ascanius (also known as Iulus, Julus, or Ascanius Julius.) He carried with him the Lares and Penates, the statues of the household gods of Troy, and transplanted them in Italy. Latinus, king of the Latins, welcomed Aeneas' army of exiled Trojans and let them reorganize their life in Latium. Aeneas had an extensive family tree including Iulus (or Julius), who founded Alba Longa and was the first in a long series of kings. According to the mythology outlined by Virgil in the *Aeneid*, Romulus and Remus were descendants of Aeneas

figure 5 - Dante

---

through their mother Rhea Silvia, making Aeneas progenitor of the Roman people. The Julian family of Rome, most notably Julius Caesar and Augustus, traced their lineage to Ascanius and Aeneas, and thus to the goddess Aphrodite. Through the Julians, The legendary kings of Britain also trace their family through a grandson of Aeneas, Brutus.

Aeneades were sodalis a (brotherhood) in a spiritual and atavistic sense and executors of the Aeneadean mission to restore the Hesperian tradition.[54]

EXCERPTS FROM THE DIVINE COMEDY[55]

Inferno

> "Ye who possess sane intellects,[56]
> aim to understand the doctrine hidden
> behind the veil of these strange verses"

Purgatorio

> "Do you not see, we are but worms[57]
> born to transform into angelic butterflies,
> who soar to justice without constraint?"
> "Why is your pride held so high, when[58]
> you are deficient creatures to a fault,
> like worms, transformation never knows?"
> "And he said to me: Because your mind
> Is still fixed on earthly things,
> of true light only darkness shows.

---

[54] Dante – Letter to Can Grande and especially De Monarchia, where Dante narrates the mystery surrounding the return of the Veltro and the Can.

[55] Dante, *Divine Comedy* – excepts from the *Inferno, Purgatorio, Paradiso* are translated by David Pantano.

[56] Dante, *Divine Comedy*, *Inferno* – Canto IX, verses 61-63.

[57] Dante, *Divine Comedy*, *Purgatorio* – Canto IX, verses: 61-63.

[58] Dante, *Divine Comedy*, *Purgatorio* – Canto XV, verses: 64-75

That infinite and ineffable goodness
from on high speeds to love
like a ray of light upon a shiny body.
So much so that it glows with ardor;
and, bestows love in equal measure,
the greater goodness grows.
The more that people love highly,
more will love yield goodness, and more will you love,
as a mirror they reflect each other."

Paradiso

"The glory of he who moves all things[59]
And penetrates the universe, shines
in one part more and in another less.
I was in the heavens that receive more light,
And I saw things that those who descend
have neither the power or the wit to say what was seen...
O great Apollo, for this last labor,
I pray, make me a vessel worthy
to be crowned with the laurel.
you will see me at the foot of your beloved wood
come, and crown me with the substance
that will make me worthy."
"A little spark ignites a great flame[60]
Better voices than mine perhaps will follow

---

[59] Dante, *Divine Comedy, Paradiso* – Canto 1, verses 1-15, *Paradiso*, Canto I, verses1-15, 25-27, 34-36,70-72, 97-99.

[60] Dante, *Divine Comedy, Paradiso* – Canto 1, verses 25-27.

> And prayers to Cyrrha plead respond."
> "To transcend the human cannot[61]
> be expressed in words, let the example be sufficient
> to grace the experience alone ...."
> "and said: "Pleased am I, to be released[62]
> from this great marvel; but now I admire
> how I transcend in these bodies of light."

In the mid-1400s, during the final years of the Constantinople-based Eastern Roman Empire, the leading Byzantium scholar and mystic, Giorgio Gemisto Plethon, set out on a mission to revive Platonic philosophy throughout Europe. In 1438 Plethon was invited to participate at an ecumenical council in Florence that attempted to reconcile the Greek and Latin churches. Through his multifaceted and erudite teachings, Plethon helped to re-introduce and spread the knowledge of Plato's philosophical corpus to scholars. Plethon's influence in Italy was considerable, especially with the prodigal Florentine scholar, Marsilio Ficino (1433–99), and with the De Medici family, who patronized the arts and sciences, and also sponsored the founding of an Academy in Florentine based on the ideals of the ancient Platonic Academy of Athens.

Marsilio Ficino of Florence (1433-99) was one of the most influential thinkers of the Renaissance. He placed before society a new ideal of human nature that emphasized man's divine potential. As teacher and guide to a remarkable circle of men, he made important contributions to the changing landscape taking place in European thought. For Ficino, the writings of Plato

---

[61] Dante, *Divine Comedy, Paradiso* – Canto 1, verses 34-36.
[62] Dante, *Divine Comedy, Paradiso* – Canto 1, verses 97-99.

provided the key to the most important knowledge available to mankind, knowledge of God and the soul. It was the absorption of this divine or metaphysical knowledge that was valued by Ficino, his circle, and by later writers and artists. As a young man, Ficino was directed by Cosimo de' Medici towards the study of Plato in the original Greek. Later he formed a close connection with Cosimo's grandson, Lorenzo de' Medici, under whom Florence achieved its age of brilliance. Gathered around Ficino and Lorenzo were luminaries such as Landino, Bembo, Poliziano, and Pico della Mirandola. The ideas they discussed became central to the works of Spenser, Shakespeare, Donne, Botticelli, Michelangelo, Raphael, Dürer, and many other writers and artists.[63]

In 1462, Cosimo De Medici embarked on re-forming Plato's Academy at Florence and chose Ficino as its head. Cosimo supplied Ficino with Greek manuscripts of Plato's works, whereupon Ficino translated the entire corpus into Latin. Ficino also translated into Latin a collection of Hellenistic documents known as the *Hermetica*, and the writings of Neo-Platonists, including Porphyry, Iamblichus, Plotinus, and Pseudo-Dionysus. In 1463, Marsilio Ficino translated into Latin the *Corpus Hermeticum*. The term applies to Marsilio Ficino's Latin translation in fourteen tracts, of which eight early printed editions appeared before 1500 and a further twenty-two by 1641. This collection, includes Poimandres and Hermes discourses to disciples Tat, Ammon, and Asclepius, which was said to have originated in the school of Ammonius Saccas and to have passed through the keeping of Michael Psellus. The last three tracts in modern editions were translated independently from another manuscript by Ficino's contemporary Lodovico Lazzarelli (1447–1500) and first printed in 1507. The re-emergence and translation

---

[63] Marsilio Ficino, *Three Books on Life*, MRTS.

of the foundational texts attributed to Hermes sparked the revival of interest in Hermeticism across Europe.

Marsilio Ficino on Divine Love

Ficino was instrumental in reviving the concept of "platonic love" in the West. He developed the concept fully in one of his most influential works, *De Amore*. Written in 1484, Ficino's philosophy of love can be summed up, as essentially referring to two primary themes, light and love.

> Light is the splendor of divine beauty. It penetrates the whole creation, and all created things, therefore, partake of it. Whenever man casts his eyes on the beauty of the universe and considers it, he sees and loves everywhere a beam of the supreme light, and is turned upward to the intuition of its pure essence. Love is the vital principle of universal existence, because love is in all things and for all things, indissolubly embracing them all: Since they are the work of a single artificer, all the components of the world, as parts of the same machine, similar to one another in essence and life, are bound together by a certain reciprocal affection. Hence rightly love may be called the everlasting knot and bond of the world, the immovable support of its parts and the firm foundation of the whole machine. Reality is seen through the eyes as form, and is felt through love to be love. In all things there is a soul; and this soul is nothing but a secret power, the principle of life and harmony, a kind of beauty. The material body is insignificant compared to the immortal soul.[64]

---

[64] Marsilio Ficino, *The letters of Marsilio Ficino*, volumes 1-10, Shepheard-Walwyn.

Ficino asserts that "only by divine inspiration can men understand true beauty." Understanding true beauty is necessary for the ascent of the soul to the Angelic Mind, and thence to God. The Angelic Mind tries to reach God through beauty, which is determined by desire. Ficino defined desire as partaking through the influence of the two Venuses and two Cupids – divine and vulgar (earthly). The platonic source for this notion of ascent is referred to as the "ladder of love."[65]

The essence of reality, then, lies inward. The truth of all things is to be sought beyond the outward veil that envelops them. Man can grasp the secret of the world. His inner eyes can pierce the dim surface of reality and see everywhere the shining imprint of God's beauty. The effort to rise, above all appearances, to truth marks the steps of man's ascent towards God: an ascent by degrees, which is a return and a re-conquest. In Ficino's *Commentary on the Symposium,* or *De Amore*, he argues that love and beauty provide the means to ascend to the divine.[66] Among artists and cultured society of the Renaissance, beauty is seen and understood as the outward manifestation of inner virtue.

Ficino was an ordained a priest, who besides performing religious rituals also practiced medicine, astrology, astral magic, and vegetarianism. Confessing to a lifelong affliction of depression, Ficino laid out in elaborate detail his personal astrological chart that showed the dominance of Saturn in his constitution. To counter this melancholic disposition, Ficino was quick to engage an Orphic lyre and churn out notes to lift his soul up to aerial regions beyond the influence of Saturn's sickle.

---

[65] Marsilio Ficino, *Commentary on Plato's Symposium on Love*, Spring Publications.

[66] Arnolfo B. Ferruolo, *Botticelli's Mythologies*, Ficino's *De Amore*, Polizano's *Stanze per La Giostra: Their Circle of Love*, Harvard University.

The Florentine Academy was an attempt to revive Plato's philosophy and influence the direction and tenor of the Italian Renaissance and the development of European philosophy. The influence of these teachings continued throughout the Renaissance, where Marsilio Ficino was known for performing astral magical practices that borrowed heavily from the ponderous tome of occult and magical doctrines, the *Ghayat al-Hakim* – better known as the *Picatrix*.

Ficino wrote the influential *De Triplici Vita* (*Three Books on Life*) in 1489, that counsel medical and astrological practices for maintaining health and vigor, as well as espousing the Neo-Platonist view of the world's ensoulment and its integration with the human soul.

> There will be some men or other, superstitious and blind, who see life plain in even the lowest animals and the meanest plants, but do not see life in the heavens or the world...[67]

In the *Book of Life*, Ficino describes the inter-connections between the spiritual and the phenomenal worlds, the links between cause and effect. He refers to a list of sidereal and psychological influences that hold sway over man's destiny. His medical works exerted considerable influence on Renaissance physicians such as Paracelsus, with whom he shared the view of the unity and correspondence between the macro and micro Cosmos, and through their somatic and psychological manifestations, which led to the study of signatures as the sign posts to interpret the nature of diseases.

Ficino's Latin translations of the *Corpus Hermeticum* revived interest in the study and practice of Hermeticism

---

[67] Marsilio Ficino, *The Letters of Marsilio Ficino*, Volumes 1-10, Shepheard-Walwyn.

in the Occident. The influence of Ficino's philosophical works and translations was immediate, through the works of his heirs; Pico Della Mirandola, Giordano Bruno, Tommaso Campanella, and continued right down to the present times. Marsilio Ficino represents the quintessential Renaissance polymath: a spiritual magus and Vates whose erudition and teachings open a new world of discovery that led to the revival of the Hermetic arts and initiatory practices in the Western inner teachings.

Pico Della Mirandola and the Christian Cabbala

> You were not made heavenly or earthly, nor mortal or immortal, because as a seemingly free and sovereign being, you have molded and shaped yourself into a form that is of your own doing. According to your will, you can degenerate into an inferior being that is bestial, or regenerate into a being that is divine – Pico della Mirandola, *On the Dignity of Man*

Following Ficino, fellow Florentine, Pico Della Mirandola (1463-94), a nobleman and philosopher, took up the mantle of a Renaissance genius by contributing several seminal texts on humanism and metaphysics such as the treatises on human dignity (*Oration on the Dignity of Man*) and free will (900 theses), and his most enduring work on a Christian-form of Cabbala, the *Heptatus*.

Pico took up residency in nearby cities of Perugia and Fratta. It was there, as he wrote to Ficino, that "divine Providence ... caused certain books to fall into my hands. They are Chaldean books ... of Esdras, of Zoroaster, and of Melchior, oracles of the magi, which contain a brief and dry interpretation of Chaldean philosophy, but full of mystery." It was also in Perugia that Pico was introduced to the mystical Hebrew Kabbalah, which fascinated him, as did the late classical Hermetic writers, such as Hermes Trismegistus. The Kabbalah and Hermetica were thought in Pico's time to be as ancient as the Old Testament. The most original of his 900 theses concerned the Kabbalah. As a result, he became the founder of the tradition known as Christian Cabbala, which went on to play a central part in early modern Western esotericism. Pico's approach to reconciling different philosophies was one of extreme syncretism, placing them in parallel, it has been claimed, rather than attempting to describe a developmental history.

In 1494, at the age of 31, Pico was poisoned under mysterious circumstances along with his friend and poet Angelo Poliziano. It was rumored that his own secretary had poisoned him because Pico became too close to Savonarola, the Dominican friar and preacher active in Renaissance Florence. Savonarola was known for his doom and gloom prophecies, the destruction of secular art and culture, and his calls for a fundamentalist Christian renewal. Pico was buried in Florence, and Savonarola delivered the funeral oration.

Ficino wrote:

> Our dear Pico left us on the same day that Charles VIII was entering Florence, and the tears of men of letters compensated for the joy of the people. Without the light brought by the king of France, Florence might perhaps have never seen a more somber day than that which extinguished Mirandola's light.[68]

In 2007, the bodies of Poliziano and Pico della Mirandola were exhumed from St. Mark's Basilica in Florence. Scientists under the supervision of Giorgio Gruppioni,

---

[68] Marsilio Ficino, *The Letters of Marsilio Ficino*, volumes 1-10, Shepheard-Walwyn.

a professor of anthropology from Bologna, attempted to determine the cause of the two men's death using modern technology. A year later, they announced their results, which showed that both Poliziano and Pico died of arsenic poisoning, probably at the order of Lorenzo's successor, Piero de' Medici. Pico's nephew Giovanni Pico Della Mirandola (1470-1533) furthered the exposition of inner traditions with an erudite study on the alchemical fabrication of gold, in his text, *De Auro*.

Pomponio Leto and the Roman Academy[69]

Sigismondo Malatesta, Condottiere (lord) of Rimini, was an important patron of humanist culture in the Renaissance. He is best known for defeating the Ottoman armies (in 1464), and for building the famous "Malatesta Temple" extolled by Ezra Pound in the *Cantos*. As a patron of scholars, Malatesta was in contact with the "Accademia Romana" (Roman Academy) founded by Pomponio Leto (1428–1498). In 1457, the humanist scholar Pomponio Leto set about to revive classicism and establish a tradition of ancient Roman gentility. Leto founded the Roman Academy, whose members adopted Greek and Latin names such as Callimachus, and met at Leto's Villa on the Quirinal. Members of the Academy visited to discuss classical and humanist life, such as the annual ritual to celebrate the founding of Rome (April 21) and to commemorate its first king Romulus. The Roman Academy's constitution resembled that of an ancient priestly college, with Laetus nominated as Pontifex Maximus, and taking on the Latin name, Iulius Pomponius Leto. The Academy promulgated ancient roman and

---

[69] Pomponio Giulio Leto and the Roman Academy – Maria Accame Lanzillotta, *Pomponio Leto: vita e insegnamento*, Tored.

humanist works such as the publishing of Vitruvius' *De Architectura* and having staged the first production of a Senecan tragedy since antiquity. The Academy received a dispensation from Emperor Frederick III to invest the best poets of the day with the laurel wreath. Under the suspicion of restoring pagan religion, the Roman Academy was shut down by the Inquisition.

In 1498, the same year of Leto's death, the Hermetic Orders of the "Fratres Lucis" and the "Fratres Tenebris", were founded in Florence. The initiatic orders were of Neo-Pythagorean inspiration and were immediately condemned for heresy by the tribunal of the Inquisition. Following the example of Dante and the Fedeli d'Amore, members of the Order were secretly referred to by the symbolic name of "Sister."[70]

In 1515, Giovanni Aurelio Augurelli (1454-1537) wrote an influential treatise on the art of making gold called the *Chrysopoeia* which was reprinted on multiple occasions times and translated into several languages. Like the majority of Renaissance humanist literature, the treatise allegorizes the classical myths of heroes to represent the alchemical operations of *solve et coagula* (filtering and refinement). This is done by using mythological content as the source material to represent the various stages of transformation undergone by the Hermetic hero, and by transposing the sublimation of the self in the face of existential challenges onto the process of sublimating gross energies into subtle ones. Giovanni Braccesco (1482-1555) was an alchemist from Northern Italy who wrote about the elixir of long life, in *The Exposition of Geber* (*La esposizione di Geber*) and *The Wood of Life* (*Il legno della vita*).[71] Braccesco's treatises greatly influenced the

---

[70] Fratres Lucis – Melita Denning, Osborne Phillips. *The Foundations of High Magick: The Magical Philosophy*, Llewellyn Publications.

[71] Giovanni Braccesco, *Il legno della vita dale edzione*, 1562, Edizioni

twentieth century Italian philosopher of Hermeticism, Julius Evola, as evidenced by the numerous citations from Braccesco's works in Evola's *The Hermetic Tradition*.

The Hermetic philosopher Giulio Camilo (1480-1584) closely followed the activities of Pomponio Leto's Roman Academy to revive the humanist culture of ancient Greece and Rome.[72] Giulio Camilo was recognized as a master of mnemonic practices (art of memory) who in his still relevant work *The Theatre of Ideas* (*L'Idea del Teatro*), which articulates in great detail mnemonic techniques to empower the mind by designing an internalized theatre of the universal mind.

Francesco Colonna & the Hypnerotomachia Poliphili

Perhaps the most elaborate expression of mystical love in the Renaissance was articulated in an enigmatic work entitled the *Hypnerotomachia Poliphili*. The title is taken from the amalgamation of several Greek words – Hypnos/sleep (Ύπνος), Eros/love (Ερως), and Mache fight/strife/struggle (μαχε). The text was written by an unknown writer who some claim was an obscure Venetian monk. However, the most convincing research attributes this work to Francesco Colonna (1433–1527), scion of one of Rome's oldest aristocratic families and whose pedigree claims descent from the Julian gens (Aeneades stirpes). The first edition of the book was released in 1499 by the celebrated Aldine Press of Venice, renowned for printing classical Greek and Latin books. The *Hypnerotomachia* went through several editions and re-prints as a result of the notoriety it quickly gained as much for its peculiar

Rebis, 2011.

[72] Giulio Caillo Delminio, *L'idea del theatro*, Con "L'idea dell'eloequenza", "De transmutation" e altri testi inediti, Adelphi.

story as for the elaborate illustrations which depict scenes of nymphs in various stages of erotic desire. *Hypnerotomachia Poliphili* is a curious read due to the arcane subject matter that surfaces in the form of allegories vested by the veils of pursuits and struggles of the central protagonist, Poliphilo for the object of his love, Polia, which symbolically refers to the union of his Lunar and Solar selves (Polia with Poliphilo).[73] The journey, not unlike that which we've seen referenced in the Virgilean or Dantean katabasis involves an oneiric submergence into an altered state of consciousness where the protagonist (initiatic hero) navigates through mnemonic, oneiric, imaginal, mythopoetic, and architectural landscapes. The book is replete with protean scenarios which the author is able to recall through the aid of mnemonic techniques that reference archetypal signifiers in the form of Olympian divinities, heroes, and spiritual initiations set against a backdrop of architectural reference points (*loci*). Poliphilo's journey culminates in the reconciliation with his beloved Polia by the "Fountain of Venus", which sparks a vision of the goddess Venus. The narrative flows jaggedly in a stream of consciousness manner with numerous twists and spontaneous tropes, as one would experience in a turbulent dream. Here the contents of the unconsciousness are projected outward in the form of universal images onto the simulacrum of the inner eye where seemingly unconnected and incongruous images are woven together in a rich menagerie of themes. In many aspects the form of expression resembles the phantasmagoric works of twentieth century Dadaists and Surrealists. Yet the underlying cycle of meta-themes is similar to those in which we've encountered in the

---

[73] Union of solar and lunar selves – in Western Hermeticism this state is referred as the perfect union or integration of male and female energies of the Self leading to a state of self-sovereignty. *Hermetic Dictionary*.

works of Vates like Dante and Virgil that speak of a man who descends into the underworld and undergoes trials that test his character. In the case of Poliphilo, the trial associated with his journey in the underworld is represented by the incompleteness of his character, manifested by the state of torpor and emasculation of his will, and the paralysis of his psyche to adequately respond to the oneiric snares of Hydra-like entanglements. Yet through this struggle and strife, Poliphilo triumphs by his mastery of the initiatic arts, e.g. an atavistic resurgence of the Julian stirpes: virtues of strength, memory, and oneiric will-power, to re-integrate his Lunar and Solar selves into a union where the whole is greater than the sum of parts. Poliphilo avails of the many trials and through his newly gained powers, is able to re-affirm himself, gain strength, ingenuity, and to complete the metamorphosis into a hero.[74]

EXCERPT FROM THE HYPNEROTOMACHIA POLIPHILI[75]

Lector, if you wish to quickly understand what this work entails, know that Poliphilo recalls in great detail, many wonderful things seen, which he calls in the Greek vernacular "The Strife of Love in a Dream."

Poliphilo professes to have seen many ancient objects worthy of memory. And all that has been told, in great

---

[74] Oneiric triumphs.

[75] Francesco Colonna, *Hypnerotomachia Poliphili*, M. Ariani (a cura di), M. Gabriele (a cura di).

Leon Battista Alberti's *Hypnerotomachia Poliphili*: Eros, Furore and Humanism in the Early Italian Renaissance.

Il Sogno di Polifilo – Maurizio Calvesi, Officina Editore, 1980. Francesco Colonna, *Hypnerotomachia Poliphili: The Strife Of Love In A Dream*, Thames & Hudson, 2005.

detail and described in his own words with elegant style:

pyramids, obelisks, decayed buildings lying in ruins, various column types stripped to dimensions, capitals, bases, letters with rectangular beams, inflexed beams, zophorae or frises, and columns adorned with furnishings.

A great horse, a large elephant, a colossal statue, a magnificent door made to measure with sublime ornamentations ... a sudden frightened scare, the ominous presence of five Nymphs, a magnificent bath, fountains, a palladium for the queen who personifies free will, an extraordinary meal fit for royalty;a variety of zoie or precious stones and their properties; a game of chess played out as a dance in three scaled notes.

Three gardens, one of glass, one of silk, another as a labyrinth, that represents human life.

A lateral peristyle, which in the middle ages represents the Trinity with hieroglyphic figures, such as that which is found in sacred Egyptian sculpture.

There are three doors that Poliphilo, as was his custom, would pass through along with Polia.

Polia leads him towards four triumphs of Jove, the amours of the gods, and those of poets, the effects and affections of divine loves.

The triumph of Vertumno as Pomona. The ancient sacrifice of Priapus.

A marvelous temple for descriptive art, where sacrifices are performed as admirable rituals and religious celebrations.

Poliphilo and Polia venture to the coast and await the arrival of Cupid, amid a ruined temple, Polia persuades Poliphilo, to admire the ancient vistas, and the many epitaphs, such as an inferno depicted in a mosaic. And suddenly overcome with fear, he flees from there only to embrace Polia, Cupid appears on a boat drawn by six rowers of Nymphs, whereby Poliphilo and Polia are stirred, then Amor lifts her wings and flies away...

Ludovico Lazzarelli and Giovanni Mercurio Correggio

Ludovico Lazzarelli (1447-1500) was a follower of the itinerant preacher, Hermeticist, and bon-vivant, Giovanni Mercurio da Correggio. In the mid-1400s Florence was an important tributary for the diffusion of Hermeticism throughout Renaissance Italy. Lazzarelli translated the *Corpus Hermeticum* into Latin and included different codices of the *Hermeticum* that were not previously translated by Marsilio Ficino. In the manner of a true renaissance man, Lazzarelli was a humanist, poet, philosopher, alchemist, practicing magician, and augurer. Upon arriving in Bologna, Giovanni Mercurio Correggio was arrested for heresy, and forced to flee the city. The writings of the two Hermeticists are not without lasting merit as attested by the German sapient, Heinrich Cornelius Agrippa, who liberally quotes sections of Lazzarelli's *Crater Hermetis* in his *The Three Books of Occult Philosophy*. It was during this time, that in Rome, Correggio proclaimed himself to be a "young Hermes," implying that he is either the son or reincarnation of

Hermes Trismegistus, hence the adoption to his name of "Mercurio".[76]

The pomp and exuberance of festivals, ceremonies and events was celebrated throughout Renaissance Italy. Sponsored by princes and clergy, the large-scale enactment of carnivals and processions provided a forum of street theatre for the people in the cities and towns of the Italian peninsula. Carnivals were accompanied by triumphal processions that included men in costumes, emblems, wedding celebrations, and banners that portrayed heroic, dynastic, allegorical, and cosmological themes. This form of street procession had its roots in earlier Roman parades from the classical period, that celebrated military, political, or religious triumphs. Triumphal processions of this kind flourished across Renaissance Italy during the 14th and 15th centuries and may have provided the original inspiration behind the appearance of the oldest Tarot Triumph cards, the Visconti-Sforza. These cards were designed by artisans and depicted in pictorial format Olympian themes, mythological figures, local princes, and popes celebrated in the processions.[77] The Visconti-Sforza triumphs are the oldest surviving tarot cards and date back to a period when the tarots were still called *Trionfi* ("triumphs" i.e. trumps), and used for everyday playing. They were commissioned by Filippo Maria Visconti, Duke of Milan, and by his successor and son-in-law Francesco Sforza.

The forces which shaped the development of Tarot imagery and iconography were products of the imagination that tapped into the archetypal reservoirs in the collective memory of Italians and which resurfaced as a result of the (triumphal) processions, triggering a resurgence of atavistic forms of expression.

---

[76] Ludovico Lazzarelli, *Opere Ermetiche*, Fabrizio Serra Editore.

[77] Origins of the Tarot in the Italian Renaissance – Cherry Gilchrist, *Tarot Triumphs*, Weiser Books.

DAVID PANTANO

Giordano Bruno on the Sigil of Sigils

Here, under a human rind, feral animals are hidden. Should a beastly soul inhabit a man's body as if it were a blind and deceptive home? What are the laws that govern nature? ... I adjure you, for the lame ministers who protect the face of errors, for the high power of the keepers who are guardians of nature, snatching from each bestial individual the appearance of human beings, let these beings show themselves to their outward and truthful figures. – Giordano Bruno, *Cantus Circaeus*.

Giordano Bruno of Nola (1548–1600) wrote extensively on philosophical, scientific, and metaphysical subjects. His treatises include works on cosmology, astronomy, cabala, numerology, mnemonics, and magic. He is best known to the English-speaking world as a martyr for free thought who was burned to the stake in 1600 by the Inquisition amid accusations of heresy. Bruno's philosophical corpus of works gained popularity in the English-speaking world during the nineteen sixties as a result of two academic yet popular books by Dame Frances Yates – *Giordano Bruno and the Hermetic Tradition* and *The Art of Memory*. Bruno's writings on natural magic elaborate in great detail the techniques employed by the Hermetic operator or magus to exercise the "magic of love" (Ars Amatoria). The magus is the individual who intimately understands the universal laws of sympathy and antipathy, the causes and effects of manipulating the forces underlying those laws, and the forms or images by which they appear. The Renaissance magus was a master of applying the practical aspects of the Ars Amatoria, which was first articulated by Ovid, and subsequently, by a long list of practitioners from Dante and the Fedeli d'Amore poets to Marsilio

Ficino, and through to Francesco Colonna. To achieve the intended outcomes, the magus must learn how to make and effectively project phantasms (*umbrae*, universal images) to bond or enchain (*viniculum*) the imagination of the intended receiving parties. The psyche was understood by the Renaissance magus, not as a physical organ, but as a power with unlimited potentiality.

> Magic is an universal and organic language, that in its purest form becomes the expressive and productive vehicle of the will and by exercising their operative processes "men can become cooperators of the great activity of nature." – Giordano Bruno, *De Magia*.

Bruno learned the art of memory as a twelve year old boy, by studying Pietro da Ravenna's treatise on artificial memory called *The Phoenix* (*La Fenice*, 1491). He would refer to the experience as "a flame, whose sparks continue to kindle over time, able to light the prairies of my mind." Bruno taught the Art of Memory throughout the courts and universities of Europe, often showcasing his prodigious powers of recall, combinatoric logic, and articulation that fueled his growing notoriety as a formidable magus.

Bruno's third work on the Art of Memory, *The Sigil of Sigils* (*Sigillus Sigillum*) references a set of sigils, which represent the psychodynamic structures for arranging and constructing images in the mind and for processing mental representations and propositions used in mnemonic recall. In this work, the Nolan combines both the retrospective art of memory and the prospective art of logic originally developed by the medieval Catalan sage, Ramon Llull. Appended to his book, *The Sigil of Sigils*, is a treatise on the powers of the psyche from a Neo-Platonic viewpoint.

To memorize anything, Bruno implores, requires the ability to imagine vivid, emotionally stirring images and distribute them around a piece of familiar architecture. This is the method of *loci*, or the memory palace method, first developed in classical antiquity. Giordano Bruno perfected the art in the late 16th Century. He published a series of books on the subject, beginning with *De Umbris Idearum* (*On the Shadows of Ideas*).[78]

Bruno expanded upon the Art of Memory as a tool not only to foster memory, but also to project intelligence through the agency of encapsulated ideas into sigils (figurative images) that are internalized in the psyche (umbrae = shadows) and unconsciously projected outwards as vectors of the will. The formulation of sigils or internalized signs consist of geometrical diagrams, universal images, or archetypal figures reduced to their primary factors and configured with properties or virtues inherent with the sign. Bruno references the magical properties of mathematical procedures:

> In the basic system of the classical Art of Memory, also known as the method of loci or memory palaces, you must follow a basic set of rules. To remember anything, convert them into images and then distribute those images in a set of places around a building or other structure in a sequenced order. To retrieve those images, retrace your steps through the sequence of places, viewing and decoding each of the images as you go. The places should be well lit, not too far apart nor crowded together, and distinctive from one another. The whole structure should be clearly visualized. The path you take should be obvious, so you will not get lost, and to facilitate retrieval. There is also advice on how to make the images themselves

---

[78] Giordano Bruno, *Opere Magiche*, Adelphi.

as memorable as possible. They should be visually striking and emotionally resonant. (They may be terrifying, inspiring, or humorous.) They should be visualized as clearly as possible. The images should not blend into the background of the places. If a thing that is to be remembered, is not easily visualized, then you may choose to encode letters or syllables of the name of the thing into a set of predetermined images.[79]

Combinatoric logic utilizes letters and graphical representations for basic concepts to guide the mnemonist through a series of logical operations. The combinatoric logical system was first introduced into the west by the Catalan philosopher and mystic Ramon Llul (1232–1315 AD). Bruno couples this combinatoric art with the retrospective Art of Memory to construct a comprehensive psycho-computational model capable of handling every and any function. Several of the sigils resemble what modern programmers would call data structures and algorithms, while also representing functional components of a developmental memory palace. The Tree, for example, consists of a main "trunk", with secondary "branches" representing subsidiary aspects. There are other sigils, including Quadratic Wheels, that function in an analogous manner to hierarchical data structures. The sigils are constructed in multiple formats and arrayed according to the associated rules of geometry, mytho-poetic images, alphabetical and numerical sequences, etc. The images don't always align exactly with their descriptions, and sometimes they may be re-purposed as place holders to put other images in, such as microstructures at particular "places" within a memory palace that hold multiple "images" in a particular arrangement, or as primary images that contain complex ideas.

---

[79] Giordano Bruno, *Opere lulliane*, Adelphi.

The combinatory logic inherent within the construction of Sigils[80] is similar to the properties found in number theory, such as the pregnant or bountiful properties associated with Abundant numbers.[81] For this reason, the magus when formulating a sigil, must be aware of the surface significance in order for it to assist with mnemonic recall. More importantly, he must also know how to activate the inner powers or virtues which the sign conceals and by these Hermetic properties, ultimately release the binding factor to snare through sympathetic reciprocity the receiving parties. Sigils, when psychologically charged, have the power to impact and imprint the unconscious mind of sympathetic parties. The sigils are internalized in the operator's psyche by visualization techniques and consciously placed in mental storage spaces that replicate the configuration of familiar architectural, figurative or celestial locations (loci). This practice fortifies the operator's capacity to recall and communicate images at will and is known in art as the power of projection. In the Nolan's magical works, he combines the Art of Memory with the Llullian art of combinatorics to refine consciousness to the point where it becomes a vehicle for achieving gnosis in the form of ecstatic inspirations, visions, and dreams.

The dream, whether it is intended mystically as a divine language or as a vehicle for creative inspiration, is an operation of the soul "sine corpore." When closed to the "external senses", the imagination of the "inner man" frees itself from the earthly bonds in a potentially inventive "contraction."

---

[80] Giordano Bruno, *Il sigillo dei sigilli*, I diagrammi ermetici, Mimesis.

[81] Giordano Bruno, *Opere mnemotecniche*, volume 1 & 2, Adelphi.

Abundant numbers – *rara avis* in the list of numbers. A number whose sum of its dividers are greater than the number itself. For example the number 12 is 6,2,4,3,1 = 16 >12.

As such, the art of dreaming was considered highly prestigious throughout the entire Renaissance.

> The *Sigillus* is a theoretical exposition of the basic principles that regulate the art of memory, mnemonics. This text should be considered associated with the two others published in the same volume, containing a series of symbolic images, sigils, which lend themselves both to be used as mnemonic support, and to graphically represent the structures of reality.[82]

These two texts are in fact an exposition of the mnemonic principles and techniques in the form of propositions (thirty in number), accompanied by illustrations, figures, and diagrams that the author defines as "semi-mathematical".

> By virtue of the great daemon (which is love) through the spirit, the soul joins the body, and the soul joins the spirit as a more separate and divine force, and through a more or less greater number of intermediate entities all things in the universe are connected and linked to all the others. (*Sigillus sigillorum*, II.5)

There is no supremacy of the divine faculties over those of the body, as claimed by Marsilio Ficino, whom Bruno refers to in regard to this subject.

Both being and knowing are aspects of the One: the being that is, is also that what it knows, the differences are of a quantitative, not qualitative nature: knowledge is manifested in different ways according to the nature of the subject. The philosopher concludes by writing that when freed from the world of the senses, and proceeding through the intermediate degrees of the cognitive process,

---

[82] https://it.wikipedia.org/wiki/Sigillus_sigillorum

DAVID PANTANO

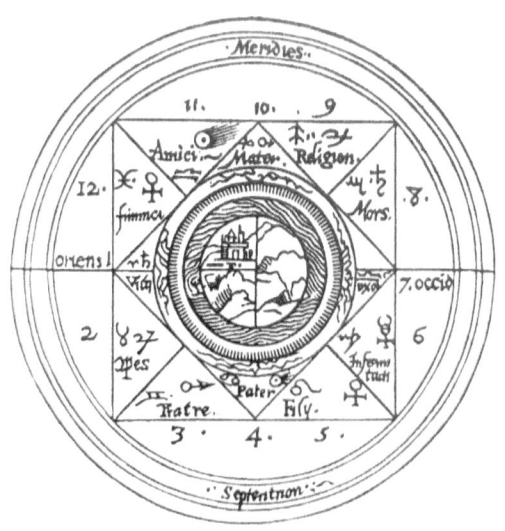

one arrives at the world of the intellect, thus abandoning "every discursive process", so one can finally capture everything in a "single act".

The unity of such a vision will have as its effect the unveiling of the sigil of sigils in its fourfold effect: discovery, disposition, judgment, and memory.

THE SIGIL OF SIGILS

Among the other things, that the Divine spirit has imprinted in me, which never rests among unclear minds; to you who hesitate and you who are inflamed toward the same things that you state in principle, so that as if from the externally excited you are incited internally, to worship God first and foremost, and that you always express that which is intended in principle, that which the numen invokes and light admires.

1. That divine spirit, which never dwells in sordid intellects, suggests to me among other things: to first of all that you understand, before attempting and becoming too passionate for the topic, this principle, that you must honor God first and closest, to magnify as sovereign, and invoke as a numen and observe like light that same entity from which you become externally excited and inwardly incited.
2. Remember that in every human activity there must be three elements: firstly, individual enterprises must be meditated upon wisely before their realization; secondly they must be completed on time and promptly; thirdly, that which has been meditated upon and completed must be maintained and defended with pride.

3. Therefore, antiquity has handed down to us that three gods preside over all activities; Pallas, Vulcan, and Mars. This is, so to speak, a trinity of "productive" gods, they always assist Jupiter, the supreme architect of the world, who, as the trinity assists Jupiter, so Vulcan and Mars assist Pallas.

4. Remember that Prometheus was not liked by the gods because, spreading the treasures of the gods, he seemed to push mankind towards slothfulness, or because he equally distributed, extraordinary gifts to those worthy and those unworthy, without distinction.

5. So always keep with you, the taste of a little of this healthy nectar, with which, once you have purified the lethargic humors from the river Lethe, you will first of all attain with certainty celestial life with the celestial gods; then you will ascend up through the super-celestial circle with the super-celestial gods, from where you will contemplate below Carneade, Cinea, and Metrodoro (Ancient Greek Skeptic philosophers), who lie with the dull vulgar lot and who no longer stand upright.[83]

Cesare Della Riviera & The Magical World of Heroes

By the early 1600s, the end of the Renaissance was in sight and the auspicious appearance of a curious treatise on the philosopher's stone entitled *The Magical World of*

---

[83] Giordano Bruno, Le ombre delle idee—Il canto di Circe—*Il sigillo dei sigilli*, a cura di Nicoletta Tirinnanzi, introduzione di Michele Ciliberto, Milano, BUR, 2000. Giordano Bruno, *Il sigillo dei sigilli*, in Le ombre delle idee – Il canto di Circe – *Il sigillo dei sigilli*, traduzione e note di Nicoletta Tirinnanzi, BUR, Milano, 2008. Frances Yates, *Giordano Bruno and the Hermetic Tradition*, University of Chicago Press.

the Heroes (*Il mondo magico de gli heroi*) by the Savoyard Baron, Cesare della Riviera, Marquis of Poncallieri and Knight of the Great Cross of Savoy, was a promising sign for the transmission of Hermeticism from one era to another. The treatise was first published in 1603 in limited edition by a small publisher based in Mantova that quickly sold out upon release. A second edition was published two years later in 1605 where it was well received by connoisseurs of Hermetic literature. Dedicated to the Duke of Savoy, Carlo Emmanuele the First, this treatise elaborates in highly cryptic and enigmatic language a process for inner transformation leading to the conquest of a Second Tree of Life. The book's short bout of fame quickly faded into oblivion and it was rarely mentioned again by the literary world. Through the fastidious research of the Italian scholar Julius Evola, *The Magical World of Heroes* was re-discovered and given a second lease of life. In 1932 Julius Evola reissued the book, translating the arcane language of the original work into a modern vernacular for the prestigious publishing house, Laterza of Bari. The eminent French scholar, Rene Guenon, was quick to write a review of *The Magical World* where he took Evola to task for modernizing the text and held reservations about Evola's statements claiming the work to be a clear and facile exposition of the enigmas associated with the Great Work and the conquest of the "Tree of Life". It wasn't the first or the last time that Guenon and Evola would duel over the symbolic interpretation of esoteric matters. With respect to this specific case, one would have to side with the Frenchman on most of his criticisms.[84]

The Magical World of the Heroes is an enigmatic, if not cryptic, treatise on spiritual alchemy that indicates a path to conquer the Tree of Life and transform man

---

[84] Cesare della Riviera, *Il Mondo Magico degli Heroi*, Edizioni Mediterranne.

into a being worthy of the divine. In the treatise, Della Riviera provides enigmatic instructions on the arcane techniques of spiritual alchemy, that were in circulation among certain aristocratic circles during the Renaissance. Della Riviera posits contemplation as the final stage of the spiritual process of alchemical purification and distillation. According to Della Riviera, the phenomenal and the visible can only offer "metaphorical" knowledge to the extent that it can intrinsically translate into the broader spectrum of human language.

If the first Tree of Life embodies a perfect identification between things and words, the second Tree of Life signifies the representation of a pristine and natural wisdom. Della Riviera emphasizes the existence of a second Tree of Life, as a divine gift awarded to the worthy human progenitor of this earthly paradise. If this second tree was to truly exist, as a real reflection of the first tree, then would the seeker have to deduce that the second tree is both a mental and memorial construct? It is precisely through a mystical operation that the mind can experience the second image as a trace of the first tree. Della Riviera references certain Hermetical practices in commerce during the Italian Renaissance to outline a method whereby the initiate, through the auxiliary of concentrated focus on the self, contemplates the elements within, to affect a self-purification, to "burn" the elements (memories, beliefs, traumas) and allow the initiate to rise anew to a purified vision of the divine. Like Ficino, Della Riviera bases his exegesis of the alchemical practice on the direct application of the two Venus' (divine and earthy). Della Riviera's treatise presents itself as the summary of Renaissance Neo-Platonic, Hermetic and alchemical thought, and Christian mysticism.[85]

---

[85] Cesare della Riviera, *Il Mondo Magico degli Heroi*, Edizioni Arktos.

Della Riviera asserts that the heroic act is the sum of initiation, whereby alchemical knowledge under the aegis of the contemplative act is the one and true process of "dissolving" the elements and ascending to higher ontological states of being. Della Riviera writes,

> "The Highest and most Liberal Factor" that created "the apparatus of the Universe", divided into three realms, the intelligible world, the ethereal world, and the dregs of the elementary world, so that it could be learned by humans through an act of contemplation and lead to the "raising of the self" to the Creator. As a fundamental guide to this work of initiation, the divine offered to human-kind the "*lignum vitae*" (wood of life).

The term "lignum vitae" refers to a process of active contemplation that potentiates the act of visualizing spiritual experiences, as articulated by the Art of Memory of Ramon Lull.

The image of the tree acts as a catalyst to set off the ascension of the mind through the celestial branches towards the divine in a process of "Angelization" of the (worthy) initiate.

That is, a mind that journeys through the various stages and branches of the meditative act to reach angelic realms.

Both the original text and Evola's modernized version[86] are in current circulation, but the original text offers a more authentic and inspiring read. *The Magical World of the Heroes* is far from being a clear and easy book, and it is weighed down with enigmas and parables worthy of a sibylline prophecy. Despite the thick hermeneutical rind wrapping the text, the work is an undeniable

---

[86] Cesare della Riviera, *Il Mondo Magico degli Heroi*, Edizioni Arktos.

masterpiece in terms of its evocative powers to attempt an explanation—by means of the classical myths of Hercules, Latona, Molly's herb, and Atheon—of a cabbalistic process of metempsychosis whereby the hero becomes both the One and the reflection of the One: the hunter and prey of the divine. This is a prime example of the merging of subject with object and the microcosmos with the macrocosmos which exemplifies the alchemical process of re-integrating the Self and the individual soul with the cosmic Soul.

CESARE DELLA RIVIERA ON THE MAGICAL WORLD OF HEROES

The highest and most liberal *factor* of all, out of nothing, creates with infinite Wisdom, the marvelous, and reduces into a great machine of the Universe, with supreme inviolable laws, that which in three parts magnificently divides; in the first, eternal and divine, called the Super Celestial world, intelligible and willed, the angelic Spirits and all of the liberated Minds; in the second, the Aetheral World, includes all of the renowned sages, heroes, and those innumerable multitudes of brilliant and luminous Celestial bodies that shine forth from the marvelous artifex; the third and last world, consists of the self-created scum and impure dregs. Finally, there remains nothing else to do, that a creature of immense *magisterium*, and great artifice of having contemplated sees; and by contemplating what he knows and loves; by loving he possesses; and thus fructifies.

Ignited by divine love and fire, by the holy name of him with whom meritorious praises are immortally celebrated: the Creator, through divine form created man; as Exemplar and Idea, not from the super celestial forms, but solely (through infinite goodness) through self exigences; having made himself through image, and similitude. This, and as his last action, then, as epilogue of the whole divine enterprise, found in the middle of the new and admirable Theater of the World: and affirmed through paternal love towards him, places his hand in the infinite abyss of creation, to enrich with infinite gifts, and prerogatives above all other creatures. And firstly, in order that man may know, in himself, the divine Image, he is assured, that as in all other things are limited by their own veritable nature, are properly enclosed, of which is not lawful to go beyond; so from no particular abstract nature, enjoys the great privilege, and from the high gift of free will, and by which through the free exercise of will, could, by avoiding certain deviations, raise himself to his Creator, and be immortal.

*****

Rejoice, to suffer from suffering like you have never suffered before: Sacrifice: that which separates – unites and that which annihilates expresses strength. A god he has become, what was once a man. – Orpheus, fragment: 20

APPENDIX

The Dominican monk Tommasso Campanella (1568–1639) is best known for heralding a new era of illumination and enlightenment contained in his revolutionary text *The City of Sun* and for writing an important treatise on applied Hermeticism, *On the Sense of Things and Magic*. His work deeply influenced the fledgling European Rosicrucian movement of the time.

The Practice of Philosophical Ecstasy

[Attributed to Tommaso Campanella (1568-1639) and excerpted from the first volume of Tommaso Campanella's Works edited by Alessandro D'Ancona, Torino 1854, English translation by David Pantano]

Seek out a place where you will not be disturbed by the glow of darkness or the glimmer of light penetrating through to the eyes, either opened or closed. Select a time when you can be quiet and released from the passions of body and soul. You should not feel hot or cold, or unease in any way, and your head should be clear from congestion, moodiness or smoke from a pyre. Your belly should not feel satiated with food rather freed from the appetites to eat, drink, relieve oneself, or of want. Sitting still, poised such that your head gently perches on your hands or in a more comfortable manner ...[1]

Clear the mind of passions and thoughts, whether they are of mercy, sorrow, cheer, fear, hope, or on thoughts of love, family, personal matters, or of other things. Neither recall memories of the past or thoughts of the present; but, having accommodated the body as mentioned above, enter into a state where you are free from thoughts that try to take hold of your mind, and when they arrive, immediately rid yourself of them, and when another one comes, right away release it to the point that they no longer interfere anymore, and finally until you've reached a state where you are no longer engaged in thought at all.[2]

In a state of complete detachment, internal as well as external, motionless as if you were a plant or stone; with the soul not engaged in activity, either vegetative or animal. Submerge into yourself, by mental means, purged of all objects of the senses, and from thought-bound discursive speech, and motionless as before, without concern of consequences: you are made into an Angel, intuitively seeing the essence of things in their simple nature, seeing the pure truth, forthright, unobtrusive, and open to the reception of answers that you propose.[3]

---

[1] The basis for a regular meditation practice requires finding the appropriate external conditions by locating a suitable place where the practitioner is at ease and is free from distractions. Internally, one should be sound of mind, self-possessed, and in perfect equilibrium of body, mind, and soul.

[2] The process whereby the Hermetic vase of the practitioner is sealed by stilling the internal energies and allowing for a convergence of vital and spiritual energies. The state of peace needs to be extended to the self; physically, emotionally and mentally.

[3] The author refers to a meditative state, known in Eastern-based practices as *Dharana* in the *Yoga Sutras*, or single pointed mindfulness (concentration) that involves clearing the mind of mental content, where discursive and aberrant thoughts are eradicated. By focusing

As you mature in this practice, you must be clear with what it is you wish to inquire or investigate, and understand, when the soul is truly purified, pose the question and then, there will appear an inner light,[4] by which truth is revealed, and with a feeling so sweet and so gratifying that there are no pleasures in this world that can compare to it; not even the enjoyment of what is most beloved and desirable, for they too fall short.[5]

After such an episode, the soul will return to the body to avail itself in the vile operations of the senses, if not, it would become greatly disturbed and would never want to return if it doubted that after the long dwelling in such an ecstasy there would not be divulged future revelations of an even greater magnitude. Therefore, the subtle spirits which dwell inside you will rise and elevate themselves to the head, triggering very sweet tingling sensations, where the mind's instruments are located: and little by little they will fade away, which if they were all to extinguish at once, would result in sure death.[6]

---

awareness on a single point (*Drshti*) and engaging in *pranayama* techniques to slow and regulate the flow of breath the practitioner will gain ascendancy over the constant flow of random thoughts.

[4] *Dhiyana* or deep-level meditation, is the process where consciousness rarefies and passes through an intermediary state of turbulence to enter a deeper state of quiescence characterized by the emergence of inner visions projected on a simulacrum.

[5] Made into an Angel, is the process where consciousness rarefies and a syzygy or conjunction occurs whereby a spiritual nucleus of conscious energy coagulates into an automatous spiritual entity able to resist dissolution.

[6] *Amrita* (ambrosia) is a special sweetness that is experienced by the practitioner as a precursor to being whisked away into ecstasy. Similar to the yogic *asana* of *Kechari Mudra*, mentioned in the *Gheranda Samhita, Hatha Yoga Pradeepika,* and other yogic and tantric texts, where the practitioner stills the mind and raises conscious energy through subtle channels to the crown of the head. By focusing his gaze on the crown centre (*bindu*), energy is intensified like a pot of water

And yet, those with a relaxed and undisturbed mind are more suited to this ecstasy, the spirits will more freely arise from the apertures.[7] Otherwise, those overwhelmed with thoughts in their head will block the subtle spirits and vital energies, rendering the exercise futile. This, I believe, is the true nature of the Platonic ecstasy, which Porphyry mentions Plotinus was abducted seven times, and he once; since it is rare that so many of these experiences can be realized in one man: it can happen perhaps thrice or four times in two or three years; and the revelations must be written down immediately and with great detail, otherwise you will lose them, and when you refer back to them they will no longer be understood.[8]

---

ready to boil. At the appropriate juncture, the practitioner rolls back his tongue into his throat cavity until the tip of the tongue is placed on the bridge of the upper mouth plate creating a surge of energy that releases a sweet sensation known as Amrita, or nectar of the gods.

[7] Alludes to the final release of the soul from the physical body.

[8] The practitioner should be prepared to quickly record the experience once he returns from the ecstasy. If not, he risks losing valuable insight from the fleeting messages that resist recollection and are susceptible to perishing in the River Lethe.

part THREE

POST-RENAISSANCE INITIATORY GROUPS

Whoever figures out why the sixteenth century thought metamorphosis was so important would make an important discovery about the Renaissance.
– Kathleen Williams, *The Gods Made Flesh*

Parts One and Two of this study outlined the contribution that an Italic form of initiation made to the Western Inner Tradition, from archaic times through to the founding of Rome and up to the Renaissance. Italic based spirituality is steeped in Olympian and Classical traditions, articulated through a mythopoetic framework. This incorporated into forms that undergo metamorphosis from human to the heroic[1] (Vir), from the heroic to the divine[2] (*Divo*[3]), or conversely,

---

[1] Vico, *On the Heroic Mind*: "So, you see, I do ask of you things greatly surpassing the human: the near-divine nature of your minds—that is what I am challenging you to reveal. "Hero" is defined by philosophers as one who seeks ever the sublime. Sublimity is, according to these same philosophers the following, of the utmost greatness and worth."

[2] Divine – Understood in broad terms as representing a transcended human condition that has realized a degree of spiritual perfection characterized by the re-integration of the Self. Examples of initiates attaining this level of being include Orpheus, Pythagoras, Apollonius of Tyra, Count St. Germain, Federico Gualdi, Cagliostro, and in recent times Ramana Maharshi.

[3] Divo, *Pythagorean Golden Verses* – "And when you have eventually divested yourself of your mortal body, you will arrive at the most pure

from human to the bestial (barbaric). The mythological narrative is privileged by the initiate for its power to feed the imagination. The imagination is the preferred *champ de cultivation* of self transformation, due to its plasticity that renders the emotional and psychic structures conducive to metamorphosis more than the somatic or hylic levels of being that are weighed down by dense laws of stasis and habitual recidivism. By harnessing the imagination (*in-mag-in-atio*), the initiate can release energies from the bonds of external senses and re-channel awareness inwards to clear consciousness of the recurring mental patterns and center on a recess of emptiness (void). However, it is by the skilled hand of the artist that the most vivid testimonies of the divine are rendered earthly. It is through the exercise of Bacchic or Dionysian arts that artist's pierce the quotidian and/or enter into enstatic states to cultivate spiritual light and yield beatific visions that translate into creative works, mirroring Giambattista Vico's[4] eternal principle: "*Verum-factum*, truth is what is made".

The Italian Renaissance is replete with artistic creations bearing the mark of the divine via the beatific vision of supernal light. One such example is Dante's *Divine Comedy* which articulates an initiatic experience from an earthly descent into an Inferno, a purgation in the *Purgatorio* and culminating with a resurgence into the transcendent realm of paradise (*Paradiso*). Admitting the inadequacy of words to express this, the divine poet invented neologisms such as "*incielare*" (internalize heaven) and "*imparadisare*" (internalize paradise) to represent the transcendent experience in common language. However, the depiction of metamorphosis through the agency of mythopoetic forms wasn't the exclusive domain of literature. Rather,

---

Æther. And you shall be a god—immortal, incorruptible—and Death shall have no more dominion over you."

[4] Giambattista Vico, *La Scienza Nuova*, Fabbri.

metamorphic representations of the divine were brought to light through artistic creations in other mediums such as painting, sculpture and architecture. Enduring examples include Botticelli's paintings *The Birth of Venus* and the *Three Graces*, Palladio's architecture consisting of Olympian temples, nympheums, and villas – or conversely Titian's painting *The Death of Actaeon* that depicts the descent of men into a bestial state of nature. Experience confirms that the ancients were closer to representing the truths of human nature than our contemporaries. Rather than limiting the human condition to simple singular or binary representations, the ancients allowed for a greater range to express the variety of orientations from semi-divine heroes like Aeneas and Romulus to brutishly depraved examples of the human species like Nero and Caligula. Not surprisingly, intermediary human-animal composites like satyrs and centaurs were also formulated, and were notorious for being wild, lusty, violent drinkers, and carousers, and generally uncultured *mal vivants*. There were exceptions of course, such as the wise centaur Chiron, who was intelligent, civilized, kind, and entrusted with the education of Achilles and Heracles in their youth. Chiron was not configured in the same manner as other centaurs, due to his heroic Numen (stirpes, ancestry). In many ways Chiron was considered higher on the ontological ladder than mere mortals for he had a more perfect *noesis/physis* or human/animal synthesis. Chiron had the head and heart of a human, and the torso of an animal.

It was through the formative prism of the imagination or *forma mentis* that the artists, poets and initiates of the classical world and the Renaissance created Western civilization's finest representations ... of the gods made flesh.[5]

---

[5] Ian Brookes, *The Death of Chiron: Ovid*, Fasti 5.379-414, Cesare Lucarini.

THE MAGIC DOOR

Figure 6 – Chiron the Centaur

Continuing on the path set forth in Part One, the following chapters examine the prominent types and forms of Italian initiatic traditions from the *seicento* (1600s) up to the cusp of the 21st century. The sections outline the contribution that select individuals and groups made to the Western Inner Traditions.

THE MAGIC DOOR OF ROME

The unbroken chain linking the Olympian spirituality of Renaissance Italy with the modern era is by way of a small yet influential circle of Hermeticists, operating in the late *seicento* (Baroque period), who were associated with the Magic Door (Porta Magica) of Rome. Also known as the Hermetic or Alchemical Door, the Magic Door was built in 1680, to serve as a gate to a villa that housed an alchemical laboratory belonging to one of Rome's oldest scions, the Marquis Massimiliano Palombara. The Magic Door of Rome is one of the few public monuments in Europe dedicated to the art of the philosopher's stone. One of five gates erected at the Marquis' villa on the Esquiline Hill, the Magic Door is the sole gate that remains intact. The Magic Door of Rome is adorned with a curious selection of sigils, that are of an alchemical and astrological provenance with associated inscriptions written in Latin and Hebrew that outline in a cryptic manner, a path to realize the Philosopher's Stone and render the initiate entry into the divine.[6]

---

[6] Nicola Cardano, *La porta magica*. Luoghi e memorie nel giardino di piazza Vittorio, Palombi.

Cesare Lucarini, *La porta magica di Roma*. Le epigrafi svelate, Nuova Cultura.

Situated on top of the gate in a circular front piece, are two overlapping triangles akin to Solomon's Seal with inscriptions in Latin: "CENTRUM IN TRIGONO CENTRI" (In the Centre of the Triangle's Centre) and "TRIA SUNT MIRABILIA DEUS ET HOMO MATER ET VIRGO TRIUNUS ET UNUS" (There are three marvels: God and Man, Mother and Virgin, the One and Three).

Arrayed in sequential manner around the door's frame are seven symbols that represent the seven visible planets and their corresponding metals, each one associated with inscriptions.

Placed on the doorstep is an inscription that reads the same from left or right, "SI SEDES NON IS" meaning both "If you sit, you won't move," and "If you don't sit, you will move." Two authors from the past century, learned in these matters, Eugene Canseliet (1899-1982) and Pietro Bornia (1861-1934), claim the signs and inscriptions bear direct influence from Michael Maier's book *Atalanta Fugiens* (1617). The seven sigils along the frame also match the illustrations found in the *Commentario de Pharmaco Catholico* by Johannes de Monte-Snyder and included in a popular book on alchemy of that time, known as the *Chymica Vannus* (Amsterdam, 1666).

The Porta Magica has received scarce attention over the past century by scholars and litterati. One of the first mentions was by the Italian esotericist, Giuliano Kremmerz (1861-1930), who lectured on the importance of the monument and stated in his book *The Porta Ermetica*, that Hermeticists would be wise to interpret the signs distinctly from the inscriptions. In other words, Kremmerz points out that the signs refer to cabbalistic operations used to enter into contact with higher planes of reality and the inscriptions refer to alchemical operations

---

Mino Gabriele, *La Porta Magica di Roma* Simbolo dell'alchimia occidentale, Olschki editore.

figure 7 – The Magic Door

associated with inner transformations. A further exegesis on decoding the enigmas of the Magic Door by Hermeticists associated with the Kremmerzian sodality the Myriam, claims that the Magic Door refers to a secret practice of initiation known as "Fire Magic" that involves magical operations conducted between two operators.

In the text *Madness as a Prelude to Fire Magic* Kremmerz provides the following insight on the Magic Door: "an infernal door, or Dantean magical door, which in various states of decomposition can be seen among the ruins of a public garden at the Piazza Vittorio Emanuele in Rome, and includes the remains of a small door adorned with cabbalistic signs that indicate how to enter through the door of Love into the optician's store, where human perception can begin to perfect itself." Furthermore:

> This derelict door that has been re-assembled in the gardens of Piazza Vittorio Emanuele of Rome, bears the cabbalistic signs of eonic magic, required to open the door closed to the profane and also a door with "inscriptions" that one should not confuse with the "signs", because the former belong to eonic magic and the latter to the great transmutatory or alchemical magic.[7]

He further states that the signs represent the seven astrological planets, or the seven attributes of the fluidic body within each human being. Of these signs only one—Venus—is identical to the traditional one. The other six are different, some more than others, from traditional astrological iconography.[8]

---

[7] Giuliano Kremmerz, *La Porta Ermetica*, Edizioni Mediterranee.

[8] Giuliano Kremmerz, *La Porta Ermetica*, Edizioni Mediterranee.

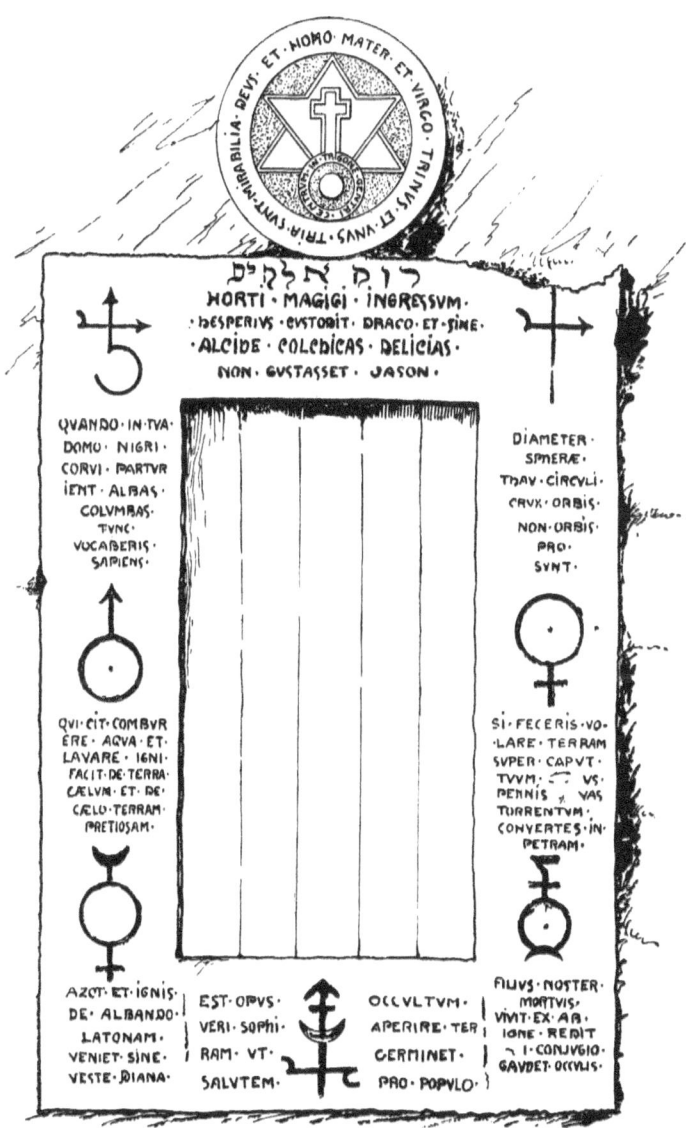

figure 8 – Alchemical Symbols

Mars, rather than this ♂ is traced this way ⚦
Mercury, rather than this ☿ is traced like this ☿
Saturn, instead of ♄ so is traced this way ♄
Jupiter, instead of ♃ so is traced this way ♃
Apollo, instead of ☉ so is traced like this ☥
Luna, rather than ☽ this is traced like this ⚶

figure 8a – Symbol Differences

Why is this the case? The answer seems quite obvious: the seven signs do not only symbolize the seven planets in the fluidic body of an individual, but also, the seven planets in the fluidic body of each of the two operators (male and female) practicing eonic fire-magic (*pyromagia*). In the fluidic body of these two operators, Venus fulfills her specific role and does not change. But the forces that Venus arouses, accumulated through the practice of continence (physical and psychological abstinence from sexual activities) following a regimen of eonic fire-magic, modifies the other planets, in an homologous manner, both in the fluidic body of the man and in that of the woman. This modification is affected through the reciprocal influence of the respective fluidic bodies exalted by Venus. This is the "eonic door" to pass, if successful, to reach the "great transmutational magical door". The state aroused by eonic fire-magic can result in the realization of different phenomena – telepathy, divinatory, etc. However, by lingering on the phenomena and dwelling too intensely on the operation, is of little immediate utility and can result in negative outcomes. In fact, the state aroused by eonic fire-magic inevitably tends to vacillate over time. If the practitioners, by deep study of a few selected texts, wisely and organically pursue the exploration of the alchemical arcana (mysteries), they can intuit and discover their secrets: even though, they are by nature enigmatic. However, if these *arcanae* are not pursued with caution or haphazardly managed, then the practice will deteriorate without fruition.[9]

The inscriptions are carved on the door that is called "infernal" and "lowly." They must therefore be read starting from the bottom, and then in an upwardly clockwise direction. We shall examine them in a loose translation, as follows:

1. *Est opus occultum veri sophi aperire terram ut germinet salutem pro populo* (Such is the occult work of true wisdom to open up the earth, so that it generates salvation for the people.) The earth is "what is below." First secret: Discover it's meaning. Remember that it produces nothing of divine if it is not used in conjunction with "what is above" and as its anchor, as its projector, as its vehicle, as its repository, and as its matrix.

2. *Azot et ignis de albando latonam veniet sine veste Diana* (After Azoth and Fire have purified Latona, Diana will appear unclothed).This is the second alchemical secret to be discovered conceptually, and then surmised for its practical application. How to purify (whiten) the raw material (Latona)? What properties do you exalt during the operation to yield the requisite results? In the whitening state? It is necessary to study the Alchemical Zodiac, where the instruments and operations are identified to purify the raw material and its properties prescribed for practical applications.

3. *Qui scit comburere aqua et lavare igne facit de terra caelum et de caelo terram pretiosam* (He who can burn with water and wash with fire makes heaven

---

[9] Giuliano Kremmerz, *Scopi e Pratiche Alchemiche dell'Ordine Osirideo Egizio*, Edizioni Prometeo.

of earth and precious earth of heaven.) The third secret must also be discovered conceptually, before delving too deeply into the practice. What is the relationship between that which in the second inscription is called: the divine entity (Diana) and what here is called water? They are the same thing! What is the "fire" that this water must ignite? This fire, ignited by this water, has the property "to wash" ... and this water: must bathe Diana. Here we discover another enigma, the secret of transmutating silver into gold. This same water (Diana) and this same fire correspond to the "two fluids of the earth" of which Kremmerz refers to in the quoted passage, where he states that the Arcana of Arcanas consists in "changing the unleavened bread, with two fluids of the earth, into a Divine entity" (the unleavened bread what can that be – does it refer to a state of being in an earthly sense, such as when the water and the fire, meld, and operate as a yeast, to transform the self into a numen?).

4. *Quando in tua domo nigri corvi parturient albas columbas tunc vocaberis sapiens* (When in your house black crows give birth to white doves, then you will be called wise). Fourth theoretical secret. The "house" mentioned here is certainly the practitioner's, which in general, one must know and master. But strictly speaking, it is the house where Diana's bath is located, that is the fire that ignites (awakens consciously) Diana and that bathes (purifies) Diana. Obviously, it is in this house (conscious numen) that Diana must make her entrance as a dove (purity). It presupposes that the "magical door" has been identified (initiation, passage into the subtle state

of consciousness - astral planes, dreamscapes, imagination, intuitions) the means by which one enters the house (by fire magic).

Placed on the highest part of the pillar, is an inscription in Hebrew – RUAH ELOHIM, "Divine Spirit"; immediately below there is a mythological reference to Jason: HORTI MAGICI INGRESSVM HESPERIVS CVSTODIT DRACO ET SINE ALCIDE COLCHICAS DELICIAS NOT GVSTASSET IASON ("A dragon guards the entrance to the magical garden of the Hesperides, and, without Hercules, Jason would not have tasted the delights of Colchis"). The alchemists identified the Golden Fleece sought by Jason in the ancient myth of the Argonauts with the philosopher's stone, the fundamental goal of their studies.

In Hermetic lore, the dragon is associated with the snake swallowing its tail; one of many symbols representing the Great Work. Hercules (Heracles) is the hero of the twelve labors and symbolizes the primordial forces (associated with the Hermetic will). Jason is the hero who conquered the Golden Fleece.

5. *Diameter spherae thau circuli crux orbis non orbis prosunt* (The diameter of the sphere, the tau in the circle, and the cross of the orbis (globe), bring no joy to the orbs (blind)). This inscription alludes to a practical realization. And since the orbs (masses of ordinary selves) are chastised, it is necessary to educate them. The tau is a letter from the Greek alphabet, signified by the majuscule letter T. The cross of the orbis is a very difficult enigma to resolve, however when you decode the arcane, it will seem obvious.

6. *Si feceris volare terram super caput tuum eius pennis aquas torrentum convertes in petram* (If you

make the earth fly over head, with its wings you may convert the torrential waters to stone). Each task has a beginning and an end. By making that which is solid (earthly, material, phenomenal) volatile and displacing it over the head (integrate with principles) that it can proceed automatically (self-projections) and pour into the currents (metaphysical channels) in which it is introduced or comes forth from. In the Great Work, the volatility of the Earth element penetrates into torrential currents (which in other texts are compared to the Nile) and represents the Water elements, and with the more ethereal elements generate the philosopher's stone.

7. *Filius noster mortuus vivit rex ab igne redit et coniugio gaudet occulto* (Our son, having died he returns from the fire a king, and enjoys the arcane conjunction). The volatile earth dissolves and the Philosopher's Stone gives no sign of life after the first alchemical work. But it lives occultly and germinates. A second alchemical operation is necessary in order to return from the fire back to the land of origin. But when the initiate returns there, he must transmute himself into a King with his kingdom in Two Lands. And with further alchemical work he will become transmuted into a Reigning Numen, whereby his castle reigns in two joint kingdoms.

In another plate, now lost, there was written VILLAE IANUAM TRANANDO RECLUDENS IASON OBTINET LOCUPLES VELLUS MEDEAE (passing by the opened door of the villa, Jason obtains the rich fleece of Medea, 1680).

The door is surmounted by a pentacle of Solomon, which is superimposed with a globe and a cross that literally symbolizes two globes with a cross, since it has two circumferences of different radius. This is of essential importance for alchemists. The globes are two, each with a cross. The problem is that the globe doesn't have a beginning or an end, or even a principle—the centre— where it is formed. However, a special inscription says: *Centrum In Trigono Centri* (In the Centre of the Triangle's Centre). And this same centre, one for each cross is symbolized by two circles of different radius. Given the symbols are in the circles within the pentacle, is there a relationship between these two circles and the pentacle of Solomon?

On the other hand, there is an affinity between the symbol "Globe with a cross", which is the "key symbol", and the Key of Isis ♀. The pentacle of Solomon also belongs to Transmutational Magic. First of all, it symbolizes the essential elements necessary for the realization of the Great Work ("That which is above" is "like that which is below" and "that which is below is like that which is above"). It also reveals the alchemical function of these elements, on all levels: "forming the miracle of the one nature". It depicts the two fluidic currents, positive and negative (male and female), which flows into the Great Work on the axis of the two poles, forming a Caduceus with each pole, and then—lightning-like—focuses its vectors on Diana.

It symbolizes the use of earthly factors in the Great Work and their projections, which is always inverse and symmetrical. Finally, it shows with perfect fidelity, the "return to the land of origin" – the operation that germinates a King (atavistic resurgence). This represents the King of the Promised Land, while reference to the 'Promised Land' correlates perfectly with the land of origin. This dual king, with an additional creative operation, is transmuted into a reigning Numen, overseeing a dual kingdom (Solar-Lunar, Rex et Sacerdotal).

Written in a circular formation around the Pentacle of Solomon, is the last inscription: *Tria sunt mirabilia deus et homo mater virgo trinus et unus* (Three are the portentous natures: God-Man, Mother-Virgin, Triune-One). These three principles are the three products of the Great Work and known as the first factors of the Great Work. The third is the last one of the triune which is the fruit of three operations. Each is a particular entity, but is also used in the second and the product of this synthesis is effused in the third.[10]

To conclude, we can refer to another passage from one of Kremmerz's writings *Madness as a Prelude to Fire Magic*.

> Rome in reverse spells Amor (Rome, Amor, Orma, Maro, and they were the hidden names of the occult City. When the hidden seas or the sacred labyrinths were unveiled, the perfumes from the meals dined by arbitrary practioners were smelt). This is why Dante took the initiate (Virgil) who knew and sung of the heroes, as his master and guide, to begin his journey from the infernal doors, where many events were experienced in the presence of the Father, the Son and the Holy Spirit.[11]

In recent years, research on the Porta Magica by noted scholars Anna-Maria Partini, Alessandro Boella and Antonella Galli (*L'alchimia della confraternita dell'Aurea Rosacroce*) confirm the affiliation of Marquis Massimiliano Palombara with a circle of Rosicrucians

---

[10] Giuliano Kremmerz, *Scopi e Pratiche Alchemiche dell'Ordine Osirideo Egizio*, Edizioni Prometeo.

[11] Giuliano Kremmerz, *Il Libro degli Arcani Maggiori*, Opera Omnia, Edizioni Mediterranee.

that were operating clandestinely in Rome, circa 1650.[12] The Rosicrucian Order which Palombara was affiliated with represented the Italian branch of a broader-based, European-wide movement dedicated to the renovation of humanity through a society that promoted universal peace and harmony rather than infraticidal war and strife among European nations. The Italian Rosicrucian circle included a mix of scholars, clergy, and nobles from Italy and around Europe such as Queen Cristina of Sweden and Cardinal Athanias Kirchner. Two prominent members of the circle were Francesco Maria Santinelli (1627-1697) and the German-born and Venetian-based Federico Gualdi (Friederich Walter, 1600 circa). Santinelli wrote several treatises on Hermetic alchemy, such as the *Androgynus Hermeticus* and the *Lux obnubilata suapte natura refulgens*, (Light shining forth by its own nature out of darkness) an important manuscript referenced by Hermetic orders and Masonic fraternities throughout the 18th and 19th centuries as well as by individual practitioners, such as Sir Isaac Newton. *The Lux Obnubilata* was attributed to a certain Fra Marc'Antonio Crasselame Chinese (anagram for Santinelli), and real name was deciphered in the 1970s by the Italian scholar Marco Baistrocchi. Federico Gualdi, regent of the Italian branch of the Golden Rosicrucians wrote several treatises on the Hermetic arts, including *The Critique of Death* and *On the Philosopher's Stone*. Rene Guenon, considered Gualdi (a man of legends reputed to have lived for over 400 years), to be one of the Invisible Masters (Maitres Inconnus) and Umberto Eco referred to Federico Gualdi in *Foucault's Pendulum*, as the master of masters.

---

[12] Anna-Maria Partini, *Cristina di Svezia e il suo cenacolo alchemico*, Edizioni Mediterranee Alessandro Boella and Antonella Galli L'alchimia della confraternita dell'Aurea Rosacroce, Edizioni Mediterranee.

Cagliostro and the Egyptian Rite

> In Egyptian freemasonry, man was created by God as the most perfect being, and later, because of original sin, decayed from his divine position to that of fragile humanity. But by initiation into the Egyptian rite one could, through a gradual healing practice, reach the ancient purity and exercise the ancient power over all terrestrial and celestial creatures. But it also opened the hope of realizing, with complex magical practices and a strict quarantine, the complete and perennial physical regeneration of spiritual ascesis. In other words, the immortality of the soul and the body could be achieved. The documents on the rites and practices of Egyptian freemasonry, minutely describe how to achieve such a coveted result. - Carlo Francovich, *The History of Freemasonry in Italy*

The initiatic practices attributed to the previously mentioned Italian Rosicrucian circle continued to exercise a considerable influence over the numerous Academies and Masonic lodges that sprouted across the peninsula throughout the 1700s. One such lodge, linked to the Italian Rosicrucian circle, was the mother lodge of Naples, The Perfect Union, circa 1750, and Raimondo Di Sangro 1710–1771. The inner circle of the "Perfect Union" consisted of a confraternity of twelve adepts, masters of alchemical practices, known as the Rosa d'Ordine Magno. The complex laboratory work practiced by this circle of adepts formed the nucleus of the Egyptian Rites of Freemasonry, which later branched out to include the numerous obediences affiliated with the Rites of Misraim, Rites of Memphis, Rites of Misraim-Memphis, and custodians of the secret rituals of the Arcana Arcanorum. In the late 1700s, the Egyptian Rites were established throughout

Europe, with Lodges practicing a spiritualistic form of Freemasonry. The Neapolitan ladder is a Gnostic system with strong Hermetic components, founded in Naples by Don Raimondo di Sangro, Prince of San Severo and head of the aforementioned Mother Lodge of Freemasonry in Naples and the alchemical cenacle "Rosa d'Ordine Magno." The origins of their particular form of teachings can be traced back to the symbolism of the Greek myths, from the Sibyl of Cumae to the rites of Eleusis, from the Pythagoreanism of Magna Graecia, and to the mystery cults and Egyptian Rites of Alexandria that were planted in Naples and environs with the establishment of the Temple of Isis at Pompei (circa 62 AD). In the 1760s, Prince Di Sangro sponsored the deciphering of scrolls uncovered in the excavation of the Iseum temple at the ruins of Pompeii. Di Sangro was instrumental in the articulation and transmission of a Hermetic-influenced Freemasonry, based on alchemical and cabbalistic practices, known as the Great Egyptian Order.

Denis Laboure writes that,

> Hermetic teachings (especially alchemical) were generally transmitted through aristocratic families from father to son. Hence one of the many tributaries where alchemy took root in Europe. When this social system collapsed in the eighteenth century, as a result of the French revolution and other upheavals, the Hermetic "veins" continued their path relying on other channels. The Masonic lodges, at first, tolerated by the Church, became a privileged vehicle. The Freemasonry of the Egyptian Rite practiced Hermeticism through a Masonic means. That is to say, collectively, as a companionship, each member facilitating the quest of the other.

figure 9 – Cagliostro

Cagliostro is attributed with the naming of the "Egyptian Rite". That said, we must understand his position. The Hermetic veins evoked previously have surfaced in this Rite. But they have also surfaced in other forms at different times. The Rite of Cagliostro is of particular interest to us because these Hermetic teachings are expressed in Masonic language. Cagliostro proposes a Hermeticism directly experienced in a Masonic context. This gives back to Freemasonry its character as a true spiritual path. It is clear that certain lineages address something much more powerful by the higher degrees known as the "Secreto Secretorum": techniques that invoke the guidance of Angels in a path of internal alchemy. The glorious body is the body of immortality. From Christianity (glorious body) to Taoism (rainbow body), this "new birth" is the typical outcome of any authentic spiritual path. Unlike Eastern Christianity, the Latin Church has often lost sight of this goal. But it has been preserved by Hermetic currents and Christian theosophists.

In the Rite of Egyptian High Masonry, the white dawn (or the white tunic) is the image of this glorious body. The Masonic apron represents the "clothing of flesh" that the initiate embodies while passing from the spiritual to the biological. It's not really a search for powers. Rather it is something else. There are two ways to understand this body of glory. Both are accurate because they correspond to two different perspectives.

Under the aegis of Count Alessandro di Cagliostro (1743–1795), the mother lodge of Egyptian Rite Freemasonry was established in Lyon. Cagliostro's Egyptian Rite follows a spiritualistic path with strong theurgical elements that engages the agency of mediums, known as Pupil's (doves), to invoke the presence of Angels. This practice preserved by the Copts is already present in the Bible. The apex of the Rite consists of a praxis of self transmutation and involves an intense forty day retreat (quarantine) where the initiate undergoes a complete biological and spiritual renovation. Similarly, the "Secreto Secretorum" ritual is based on complex theurgy, considered as an introduction to validate internal alchemical processes. The initiate engages in theurgical practices to enter into contact with Angels who will relay the unveiled secrets of internal alchemy to him. The "first quarantine" is described in the catechism of "Master of the Egyptian Rite". There, Cagliostro reveals the details of a practice taken from a highly arcane forty day retreat to "regenerate the degenerate man". At the end of this retreat, "the initiate attains a perfect state of being where he can truly say "I Am Who I Am", words which, according to the Bible, are those uttered to Moses, from the burning bush.

FIRST QUARANTINE – INVOCATION OF ANGELS

Having retired to a three-storied pavilion called Sion, constructed according to architecturally precise prescriptions, he will deliver himself to long hours of prayer, to works having for their goal the preparation of a sacred pentagon, and from the thirty third to the fortieth day he will communicate with Angels. He will have at this time acquired infinite knowledge embracing the past, the present, and the future and "his powers will be immense". After thirty-three days, he shall receive visible communications with the seven primordial angels and gain knowledge of the sigils and the numbers associated with these immortal Entities. "After the fortieth day, he will receive the first pentagon, which is the virgin paper on which the primordial Angels placed their numbers and their sigils" and then another seven "secondary pentagons of which seven angels have placed their sigils". By means of the pentagons, he can "hold command over the immortals in the name of God" with the "effect of obliging or ordering the aerial spirits, and of doing many marvels and miracles". This constitutes the theurgic ritual. According to Cagliostro, the specific goal is to "obtain the pentagon and become morally perfect," that is to say, psychically, according to the language of the time.

This path rests on the classic pattern of death and of rebirth. It implies a process by which the initiate dies in the darkness, where humanity originally fell, in order to be born again to a superior life. This "perfection" could be obtained by the practice of rituals where the symbolism is present from the beginning, but is not explained and illustrated other than progressively and in sections as the candidate progresses. It is the model of the ceremonies associated with the Egyptian Masonry of Cagliostro that spawned the birth of many so-called "Egyptian" Masonic rites. All of these rites owe a good share of their rituals and doctrines to Cagliostro, with whom, a continuity existed between "Egyptian Masonry" and theurgical rites. The initiate of the Egyptian rite, prepared by his Masonic work, could pass to the theurgic techniques with the feeling of natural continuity. In the first meaning of the term, the "Secreto Secretorum" is therefore the theurgical evocation of one or several angels, by means of talismans, sigils, pentagons, or other techniques. The "Secreto Secretorum," far from being an end in itself, marks the beginning of a path. Benefiting from the aid of evoked angels, the initiate undertakes a process of transmutation under the action of a heavenly fire symbolized by the dove represented at the level of the heart. The evocation permits the initiate to enter into possession of keys. It remains for him to penetrate the mystery of being able to use them in the proper way.

SECOND QUARANTINE – PHYSICAL REGENERATION

What does this mysterious text teach us? A process that we find in earlier texts, such as Cesare della Riviera's *The Magical World of Heroes* (1605). At spring, during the full moon of May, the initiate isolates himself, physically and psychologically, for the purpose of undertaking its operation, the first arcana of internal alchemical procedures. On the thirty sixth day, a deep sleep will follow. The initiate's hair, teeth, nails and skin will blacken and be renewed. On the thirty eighth day, an herbal bath will be taken with aromatic herbs. The thirty ninth day, the initiate will swallow two spoonful's of red wine and ten drops of the elixir *Acharat*. The elixirs are taken from Parcelsusian recipes.

On the fortieth day, he will return home rejuvenated and perfectly renovated. Thanks to the powers thus acquired, the regenerated man will be able to "propagate the truth, annihilate vice, destroy idolatry, and spread the glory of the Eternal". He submits to a regime whose object is the purification of his organism by the then known means: diet, blood letting, pure water, baths, and sweatings. From there he shall begin the practice of absorbing the Materia Prima, which is neither cinnabar nor potash, but rather symbolized by the medieval image of the red rose. This is the "animal stone" prepared in an *Athanor* that is symbolized by the above-mentioned pavilion (athanor). This animal stone is prepared according to the instructions of the earliest Rosicrucian tradition. The absorbed substance is dissolved (*solve*) by his oven, the source of continuous fire that is in the body. Just as the body of Hiram was in an advanced state of putrefaction when he was revived, the materials of the Great Work must be dissolved (solve), and decomposed in order to liberate their power. In order for the substance to deliver its essence, beginning from the seventeenth day the initiate ingests drops of azoth, a mixture of sulphur and mercury (neither common sulphur or common mercury), intimately and inseparably united, which comprises the philosophical mercury. By this he is rid of his coarse envelope and obtains an essence assimilated by his blood. From that moment, it weaves and nourishes the construction (*Coagula*) of a particular incorruptible body, the *soma psychikon*, the golden wedding garment which replaces the tunic of slavery with which Adam was clothed since the fall. This path will appear completely incongruous to the contemporary Freemason cut off from the Hermetic sources of his Order.

Lastly, an alchemical work is realized that is best explained by means of an analogy: In an egg, and from the point of view of an egg's constitution, distinguish the perishable part (the albumen and the shell) and the part promised to a more glorious destiny (the yellow yolk and the membrane that maintains its shape). The alchemical work involves activating the second (body of fire + body of air), since the first (body of water + body of earth) hardly survives death.

The initiate understands that he has an embryo of immortality. He must make it grow so that it becomes a body in its own right. For this, he can undertake a theurgic work, which will ensure contact with a certain transcendence. In the procedure taught by Cagliostro, it is represented by the biblical image of the seven Angels that surround the throne of God. There are criteria to rule out "contacts" that would be the fruit of the imagination. After this the alchemical work is done.[13]

The outer workings of the Egyptian Rite of Freemasonry became dormant following the arrest, trial, imprisonment, and eventual death of Cagliostro at the hands of the ecclesiastical inquisition. Later, in the first decades of the 1800s, there was a successor to Cagliostro as Grand Copth of the Egyptian Rite when it was briefly revived by Baron Lorenzo de Montemayor who had chapters throughout Italy. Cagliostro's legacy continued into the following century through the propagation of a gnostic system of theurgical and alchemical practices, including the Rites of Misraim, the Rite of Memphis, and the Rite of Misraim-Memphis. With this patrimony set, Naples became one of the most important centers in Europe where ancient forms of wisdom such as Hermeticism known as the "Ladder of Naples" and the "Neapolitan Node" (Scala di Napoli, Nodo Napoletano) were allowed to continue in relatively open forums within the humanist academies and Masonic lodges of Parthenope's *environs* (Naples).

Giambattista Vico and Ancient Italic Wisdom

By the mid-1600s, in Europe the Cartesian revolution had swept away many forms of knowledge, including Hermeticism and alchemy, that didn't neatly fit into the paradigms of a sense bound and empirical-based epistemology. In reaction to the hegemony of cartesian

---

[13] Les Secrets de la Franc-Maçonnerie Egyptienne, *Chariot d'Or Cagliostro: les arcanes du rite égyptien*, Spirit Occident. The French scholar, Denis Laboure is the author of several books and articles on Cagliostro and the Egyptian Rite of Freemasonry.

rationalism there emerged a Janus figure in the great chain of sages, Giambattista Vico (1668–1744). With a critical gaze equally fixed on the past and with insights that speak to the future, Vico was an ardent protagonist for classical wisdom and in his sweeping work, *The New Science*, courageously battled against the hegemony of phenomenology, materialism, and empiricism sweeping through the Western world at the helm of the Cartesian revolution. Vico is best known for coining the Verum-Factum principle. The principle states that truth is verified through creation or invention and not, as per Descartes, through the exclusive domain of the observation of empirical facts. What seemingly appears as two opposite forms, in reality, are two sides of the same coin, one a solar or active pole and the other a lunar or passive form of the same process of truth-making. It was this solar and heroic spirituality, that Vico sought to restore and cultivate for humanity.

As the leading member of the humanist Accademia dell Arcadia, a bulwark for propagating perennialist wisdom or *Prisca theologia*, Vico elaborated on the native Italic sapiential traditions in his book *De Antiquissima Italorum Sapientia* (*On the Most Ancient Wisdom of the Italians*) and on the art of transformation in *De Mente Heroica* (*On the Heroic Mind*). Vico writes: "The first wisdom of the gentile world, must have begun with a metaphysics not rational and abstract like that of learned men now, but felt and imagined as that of the first men, who with the power of ratiocination, were all robust sense and vigorous imagination." Vico's word for imagination is "*fantasia.*" This concept is understood as a power of the mind and related to the Latin notion of *poeta*, "a maker." The first humans make their distinctive form of wisdom through their power to form images. They transpose what they sense, think and feel into images or what Vico

figure 10 – Nova Scientia

calls "imaginative universals". This power to fix the flow of inner and external sensation in the permanence of the image allows the first humans to make forms from the imaginative powers of the mind, and to create, shape and form energy from that which they feel and imagine. In tandem with imagination (fantasia) and creativity *(ingegno)*, are development of the powers of invention *(inventio)* as the prerequisite for arriving at a certain design. Invention is necessary for the perfection of architecture and is on a par with creativity (ingegno) in significance. Looking at the meanings of invention reveals that, although its main connotation is to create from scratch, it also relates to discovery (*invenire*), which means to come upon something by investigation or accident.[14]

For Vico, the ability to think creatively originates in the imagination's capacity to translate the world into vivid images. Ultimately, the visual power of imagination is necessary in the perfection of the images that artists, initiates, and creative types form in their mind and make into art. What makes the imaginative faculty or "*forma mentis*" the paradigmatic matrix of human creation is the procedural analogy to divine knowing. Vico reaffirms this principle, written after the first version of the New Science. "Just as he who occupies himself with geometry is, in his world of figures, a god (so to speak), so God Almighty is, in his world of spirits and bodies, an architect (so to speak)."[15]

In the mid-1800s, after centuries of laying dormant but never completely buried, the ideals sown by Dante, Petrarch, and Machiavelli for a renewed and unified Italy, surfaced and actualized in historical time and space

---

[14] Donald Phillip Verene, *Vico's New Science: A Philosophical Commentary*, Cornell University Press.

[15] Donald Phillip Verene, *Vico's New Science: A Philosophical Commentary,* Cornell University Press.

through nascent patriotic movements like the Young Italy, Royalists under the Savoy banner, and even clericalists and liberals. Finally, in 1860, after several failed attempts, a military and political insurrection arose, led by an adventurer Giuseppe Garibaldi. At the helm of a thousand manned militia (the Mille), who had fought a series of battles to oust foreign powers, they progressively moved up the peninsula from Sicily to Rome where the political unity of the kingdom of Italy was proclaimed for the first time since the dissolution of the Roman empire.

The Neapolitan School - Domenico Bochini & Giustiniano Lebano

DOMENICO BOCCHINI (1775- 1849)

Alongside the more exoteric political and social forces that defined the times, there also occurred in parallel, an esoteric resurgence of the spiritual, philosophical, and esoteric roots that were referenced by Vico in his book *On the Most Ancient Italic Wisdom*. Two of the most important figures, who contributed to the spiritual *elan* that spawned a renewed interest in the Classical Misterio-sophic traditions of Orphism, Dionysium, Pythagoreanism, Egyptian mysteries, and ancient Roman cults were Domenico Bocchini and Giustiniano Lebano. Both men were leading figures in the burgeoning Neapolitan school of initiation that surfaced under the guise of Egyptian Rite Freemasonry by Di Sangro and Cagliostro.

Domenico Bocchini, alias Geronta Sebezio and Nicodemo Occhiboni, was from Naples where he had enrolled as a young man in the Faculty of Jurisprudence. Bocchini was an avid student of initiatic studies and member of the Scottish rite "The Sons of Liberty." As an adventurer with strong Jacobin convictions he partook in the 1799 Parthenopean revolution in favor of the republican side, until they were ousted by the Bourbon regime and were forced to flee Naples and enlist in the French army. During his stay with the French ranks he distinguished himself with courage and ability. In 1831, Bocchini returned to Naples, to practice law and write the periodical *Geronta Sebezio*, under the alias of Nicodemus Occhiboni, an anagram of his name. He was also known as the "old man of the Sebeto." Somewhat reminiscent of the ancient Indian river Saraswati in the Indus valley, the Sebeto was the name of an ancient river said to run underground from Naples to the Elysian Fields, which in mythological terms is depicted as "a road to immortality and heavenly after-life."

Around this time, Bocchini met Filippo Lebano, Giustiniano's father, with whom he closely collaborated in the Neapolitan initiatic orders of the Egyptian Rite of Freemasonry. In 1834, the famed English writer of esotericism, Sir Edward Bulwer Lytton visited Bocchini in Naples, and Lytton was initiated in the Neapolitan school of initiation. It was through his initiation in Neapolitan esotericism that Lytton invested the content of his popular book, *Zanoni*, on the sapiental-mysteries. However, it was under the pen name of "Geronta Sebeto", that Domenico Bocchini laid the foundations for the Hermeticism that would later be followed by Gustiniano Lebano, and with some variations by Giuliano Kremmerz. It was through Bocchini that Vico's teachings were revisited for the Hermetic exegesis of classical authors. In fact, it is through the adoption of the 'Palladian' method, which consisted of analyzing the root and the ending of words – or by way of the individual syllables that they were written, and then ascending from the literal, to the allegorical to the Hermetic, it is possible to find hidden keys to interpreting words and passages of the classical works.

Although the method can yield spectacular results, from an empirical-rationalist sense, the Hermetic exegesist must be careful not to force the interpretations of ancient books, and this can only be avoided if the words are arbitrarily extrapolated from the context in which they have been inserted. Taking into account the previous facts, and recalling both the argument and the history the text refers to, it should also be emphasized that there is an analogical correspondence between the four senses of interpretation that must never be in conflict with each other.

> Only the wise are Numens, for wisdom alone constitutes the primary divine elements, which symbolically is adored by 'mortals'. – Domenico Bocchini, *Gli Arcani Gentileschi Svelati*, Tomo III, p. 45, note 29.

THE ARCANE REVELATION OF THE GENTILES

(GLI ARCANI GENTILESCHI SVELATI)

TO THE VIRTUOUS READER

There were three ways of speaking in ancient times.

Demotic was the first:

The second was called Hieratic or even joyful:

The third in Hieroglyphs was the most august.

Vulgar was the preferred mode among common people, and understood by All: there is also the profound rhetoric of the Forum, and the prolific speeches from the Oratory with dire and robust sayings. In the other manner was the Sacred: to whom the Plebes understood not: rather born to serving, and with the plow ... to furrow the masses.

But with ciphers .... they are now known:

Revealed only to the mind of the Sage

The ideography of varying circles, is rote.[16]

GIUSTINIANO LEBANO (1832-1910)

Giustiniano Lebano was a fascinating and mysterious man. Part scholar, patriot, and literary figure, he was a member of the Neapolitan School of initiation that served as a repository to preserve and hand down, through hidden means, an esoteric vein derived from the Italic tradition and merged with the Hermetic.[17] The School gave expression to a sapiential line of arcane Tradition that is also present in the sacred poem of the *Aeneid*.

Giustiniano Lebano, alias Sairitis Hus was heir to the Hermetic Egyptian tradition of Naples, founded by Raimondo di Sangro, Prince of Sansevero from the XVIII century, who along with his father (Filippo Lebano) was a member of the Grand Council of the Egyptian rite. Due to their close ties with the Bocchini family, Giustiniano married Bocchini's niece Virginia. In 1853, Lebano received initiation into the Masonic lodge Folgore of the Egyptian Rite, of which he would later become Grand Master from 1893 to 1910. Together with other Neapolitan Hermeticists, he revived a number of initiatic circles, including the Grand Lodge Sebezia and the Neapolitan Golden Rosicrucian Order, dedicated to the Hermetic

---

[16] Domenico Bocchini – *Gli Arcani Gentileschi Svelati*, unpublished.

[17] Giustiniano Lebano – *Opere* vol. 1, Del Mistero e della Iniziatura, Victrix.

practices that gave rise to the Egyptian Grand Orient. In 1873 the archive of the Egyptian Grand Orient was transferred to the Villa Lebano.

Known for his great erudition on initiation, Lebano cultivated a large body of *cognoscenti* throughout Europe, including close ties with Eliphas Levi and his circle. Lebano possessed a private library consisting of over 2,000 rare manuscripts and over 5,000 volumes of Hermetic philosophy. Upon his death in 1910, the collection passed to his daughter, and to this day the corpus of rare manuscripts and Hermetic texts is a highly sought after treasure trove.

OF MYSTERY AND INITIATION (1ST ED. 1899)

Mystery and Initiation is dedicated to revealing the hidden meanings found within ancient cults. By emphasizing the symbolic use of language, found in the works of the author Petronius, the presence of archaic and symbolic meaning is revealed, starting with his own name: "The PETRA is the ark where the laws of Ceres were kept". The hidden sense of Petronius' *Satyricon* is clarified by understanding that "it is not a whole work, but of fragments." In the midst of this chaos, the philosopher reveals nearly all of the mystical strata hidden in the initiation: "Nor can you savor from those who are not accustomed to the knowledge of the ancient mysteries, which is not drawn from fashionable books of the foolish sapients, who dare not confront the wise, rather derive from the ancient classics, the source of human knowledge." According to Lebano, Petronius teaches his readers how to write in the sublime Mystical-logos manner—equal to Homer, Virgil, and Horace—but with the little that has been revealed so far, it creates further interest in Petronius' works, which are predominantly mystical, since Petronius began in Parthenope (Naples).[18]

---

[18] Giustiniano Lebano – *Opere* vol. #6, Del Mistero e della Iniziatura,

Giuliano Kremmerz and the Magical Fraternity of Miriam

> In creative magic, the imagination of things well defined, pictorial, chiseled in their finer and detailed particulars, is a will in action, it is creation. The imaginative power tends to exercise this form of realization of the will, to perfection. All the inner volitional activities are in the plasticized imagination of man. Imagine well and you will develop prodigious powers of the will to create. – Giuliano Kremmerz, *The Secret World*

The source of contemporary initiatic orders and esoteric schools in Italy can be traced back to the mid-1890s with the founding in Naples of the Magical-Therapeutic Fraternity of Miriam (Fratellanza Terapeutico-Magica di Miriam) in 1896, and with the publication of the journal, *The Secret World* (*Il Mondo Segreto*) from 1897 to 1899, by Giuliano Kremmerz (Ciro Formisano, 1861 –1930). Kremmerz was initiated into the Neapolitan school of Hermeticism (Scala di Napoli) through his apprenticeship under the tutelage of Pasquale de Servis (1818-1893), known in art as Izar Bne Escur and by Giustiano Lebano (1832-1910), head of the Great Egyptian Order, an inner circle of Adepts. In 1909, Kremmerz wrote a constitution, the *Pragmatica Fondamentale*, that was approved by the Great Egyptian Order, which outlines in sixty points the initiatic scope of the Fraternity. The study and practice of:

1. Sciences dealing with the occult powers of the human body, animism, mental activity, clairvoyance, telepathy, and all supernormal and spiritual phenomena.

Victrix. Of Mystery and Initiation appeared in two installments, n. 9 and 10 of Giuliano Kremmerz, *The Secret World*, 1899.

figure 11 – Giuliano Kremmerz

2. Classical documents, ancient texts, memories, alchemical and magical sciences, religions, rituals, popular traditions, mythologies, and truths concealed by the ancients or by religious and sectarian obstructions.

The Myriam was organized according to an hierarchical system of five grades that Kremmerz later regretted instituting because it all too often resulted in the wielding of personal power and egoistical polemics among hierarchs. Kremmerz advanced the articulation of esotericism by modernizing the terminology and introducing a scientific approach to verifying truth claims. He established a school to promulgate Classical, Mediterranean, and Italic forms of philosophical esotericism in contrast to the predominant Hebraic and Eastern variants popular at the time. The *Schola Philosophica Hermetica Classica Italica* (*Italic, Classical, Hermetic and Philosophical School*) and the *Biblioteca Esoterica Italiana* (*Italian Esoteric Library*) were established in the 1890s, to provide reference points for seekers to deepen their knowledge and practice of Classical and Italic forms of spirituality. The material gleaned heavily from Hermetic, Pythagorean, Platonic, and Italian sources including the philosophies of Dante, Bruno, Ficino, Vico, and the Italic Rosicrucian circle affiliated with the Magical Door of Rome.

The Fraternity of Myriam (or Miriam) is a sodality that practices a lunar-form of spirituality which includes the formation of a collective chain of initiants to exercise rituals designed to cultivate subtle energies for the purpose of distant healing. The Myriam practiced a sophisticated liturgy of rituals that engaged the use of sigils, ablutions, astrological observations, and fasting. The Lunar-based spirituality was intended to cultivate and exercise a maternal form of love (Myriam, Mary, and Isis are Lunar archetypes) or inner fire for the purpose of purifying and sublimating the four constituent bodies (elements or planes of being) of the Self: Saturnian (physical), Lunar (astral), Mercurial (psyche), Solar (spiritual), and held in balance by Hermes (consciousness).[19]

A tangible elevation of the practitioner's consciousness is realized when the external bodies (Saturnian, Lunar and Mercurial) are integrated with the sidereal body (Solar) and the vital energy (life force) fuses with spiritual consciousness. Individual transfiguration occurs with the effective purification and integration of the consciousness underlying each of the bodies, leading to a spiritual centering of the Self (being). In the Myriamic teachings, the initiate is seen as a holistic synergy of four elemental bodies: Saturn, Lunar, Mercurial, and Solar, where each body represents a specific vibrational frequency of the life force of consciousness. The Saturnian is the lowest and Solar the highest. This fourfold framework neatly aligns with the Tantric four elements or *Tattwas*. By practicing a daily ritual, the practitioner purifies each of the four bodies, by cascading conscious energy through the four layers of being. The practice requires a constant and effective purification and integration (solve et coagula) of the denser Saturnian, Lunar, and Mercurial bodies together to form a Maria body able to filter out the denser energy clusters and to integrate this aggregation of energy at the Solar level of the soul or Numen, which constitutes the primal, irreducible, and immutable source of consciousness.

Reference is made at this point to the centering of being within the spiritual realm known as the 5th element, Aether. Integration of the self within the soul (Numen), occurs once consciousness is displaced from external or samsaric bonds (*vinculum*) and centers internally within

---

[19] Giuliano Kremmerz, *il Mondo Secreto*, Edizioni Rebis.

the Numen. This state, renders a being rooted at the numinal node, where conscious energy can willfully be projected externally through the four bodies and manifest as virtues (*siddhis*). This higher state of realization makes the soul immune (to a certain degree) to external sense or mental-based influences. A lifetime of practice empowers the initiate to gain mastery over each of the four frames of energy and the matrices that allow projections through the four bodies as powers (virtues).[20]

1. The Quest begins when the will is sufficiently strong enough to quit the vulgar yet powerful currents of identification and submission to desires and instincts, that are the great devourers of fine substances.
2. The ego can be considered as a moving complex of small "me(s)" that are born and die in the wake of external events. It is only through the rapidity of change and the persistence of memory that gives the illusion of a stable and unique self.
3. Dear reader, as a teacher, I preclude you from using your vulgar logic in things pertaining to the spirit that is not vulgar and I tell you that, the day in which you will put aside your faith in human reason, you will renounce forever that which has not been modeled and perfected in universal reason, which conforms to your divine nature.[21]

Kremmerz writes:

> A purified LUNAR BODY transforms into a fluidic entity that contains the other two higher principles

---

[20] Giuliano Kremmerz. *il Mondo Secreto*. Edizioni Rebis.

[21] Giuliano Kremmerz, *il Mondo Secreto*, Edizioni Rebis.

(solar and mercurial body) of lighter substances, which potentially can separate from the physical body and result in an ANGELIC (ANGELUS means to make) formation, able to act without the need to engage the physical body. I inform you that, in our school, when the lunar body resolves into an angelic constitution, that even if it is embryonic, we call it MARIA. The operations of collective magic, analogous with the individual, have the power to form a collective MARIA of all the participants in the chain of operators and practicants. This is how I will explain to you that the great MARIA of our operating chain is the MIRIAM, which is the aggregation of forces from the prayers of all the individual lunar bodies.[22]

Kremmerz defines this inner fire or state of Mag, in the following terms:

The intermediate state between life and death, that which brings to surface the dormant and powerful exponent of man's hidden nature. It is a state of being that can only be understood by those who have direct experience with the power of this active trance. It is a self determined or willed state of trance of the shadow in all of its manifestations and results. The "Mag" is an intensive state of trance that places in direct communion our lunar, mercurial and solar bodies together, with the cosmic or ethereal matter that forms the astral current. In the intensity of the vibration produced by the contact of the human and astral currents, phenomena are manifested in the light of reality.[23]

---

[22] Giuliano Kremmerz, *il Mondo Secreto*, Edizioni Rebis.

[23] Giuliano Kremmerz, *il Mondo Secreto,* Edizioni Rebis.

In a monograph originally attributed to Kremmerz, yet certainly written by an anonymous author and bearing an apocryphal stamp, associated with a later incarnation of the Myriam there is reference made to an italic form of a cabbalistic interpretation on the myth of the nature of the original woman. The monograph alludes to the synchronicity of the transformational power of the Myriam with the evolution of a collective consciousness in society. The monograph references the evolution of consciousness from a primitive Lilith constitution that was rejected as problematic and relegated to the subconscious, which was replaced with another constitution known as Eve that was determined inadequate as a result of falling to temptation. Eve was then relegated to the spirit of external or profane consciousness. Then, through the Maria, it is seen as superseding and redeeming the Eve and Lilith states, representing the triumph of a Christ-centric or ethical conscience, and subsequently a Sophia consciousness of the holy spirit or Paraclete that represents the supernal or divine sphere of consciousness. This consciousness is liberated from the sheath of derivative attachments, identifications and other garments to resolve into a primary, foundational, and unique unit of being.

The anonymous author writes:

...with the progression from the minimum to the maximum, and from the worst to the best in man, one observes an evolution of the spirit or principle that terminates in the incarnation of an earthly man, the realization and adaptation of the spirit. From this result a series of corollaries, one more important than the other are realized. The main ones are:

- First Corollary – The human spirit (Numen) is eternal because it reproduces itself in different bodies (incarnations) that it in itself (principle) creates, that is, forms according to determined ends. Therefore, a man's spiritual nucleus can change into different bodies and casings, due to its unbroken journey as the seed of a plant reproduces itself (in other seeds). The ancient priests symbolized this principle with the sickle of Saturn, the god who devours and sows the seeds of his sons, and represented by the snake swallowing its tail.

- Second Corollary – Man is the realization of his informing spirit to the extent that every human life is on a mission determined by their informing spirit, and it is the preparation of every future life. Therefore, the happiness or unhappiness of a man corresponds to the success of their existential life realizing their informing spirit; the degree to which the purpose of their mission was realized or not you have the measure of happiness or unhappiness.

- Third Corollary – Man's spirit (Numen) manifests itself in all of his ideas, actions, and achievements and in the body that he takes on. Therefore, the guiding principle of a living being informs the complex acts of his earthly life. If the guiding principle is beneficial, human life is beneficial. Thus, all the generative virtues of a given plant materializes in the properties of its seeds.

- Fourth Corollary – The human body is an envelope of a seed (spirit) of a determined energy, that has come to him in the form of energy from the mission to which his seed is informed. In humanity or human society, they are sown with words, deeds and examples, such as found in the cases of priests, heroes, soldiers, and cowards.[24]

---

[24] Anonymous, *Lo Sputo della Luna*, Edizioni Carpe Librum. Italian writer Gaetano LoMonaco cautions readers that the text in question should be consulted with reservations, since much of the content is spurious or apocryphal.

APPENDIX

*Excerpt from The Secret World, Giuliano Kremmerz
(Il Mondo Secreto, 1898)*

UNUS, POLLENTISSIMUS OMNIUM!
(THE ONE, POWERFUL ALL)

Sun, radiant God, our Father, you, who create forms and with shadows provide relief to all visible entities in the wake of your eternal splendor, illuminate with your Divine light the one who, pure of mind and heart, reads in this book the laws and practices that will raise him to the power of the Numina: let him understand and not be mistaken: bestow upon him humility that he may know his ignorance and virtue to ignore the dull sensitivities of earthly life, so that the voice of the Beast seduces him not, and that he may feel the breath of your fruitful spirit.

O Sun, you, who sweep away the dark stupor from the great night of phantasms, specters of the wildest desires, superb creations of human pride, illuminate the ignorance of he who, in a world desiring temporal things, is thirsty for Eternal truths and let the Idolatry of the beast, chained to the vanity of ignorance, hear your divine ray and prepare for the advent of Christ.

O Sun, blazing God, forgive those who read my words in bad faith, to the ignorant Masons, to the preachy and blind priests, the doctors of theology who understand not the logos of your spirit, the wise worshipers of phoenic acids, microbes and serums, the critics who are clueless and to the howling screeches who are afraid; Let your messengers of Light, winged angels, and horned demons, convert them to the intelligence of the truth of visible entities.

But you, o Sun, who hide your light only to the blind, do not deny your rays and your providence to those who reading this without the virtue of the soul and of the heart, ask for proof, solely as a condition for converting to the truth. But if the proof is lacking and the tempter of the Gods, obstinate, asks again without faith, be merciful as you are magnificent. Forgive the fragility of the presumptuous. Let not your red demons blush their veins with blood, and do not allow their brains to percolate with madness before the wandering and fleeting images of desires for the non-existent.

Forgive, o Sun, and spare your terrible wrath to the blind conductors of the blind, to the Sophists and the jesters of human wisdom. While they deny, the Cock crows, and the Dawn of the Light of souls, of the intelligences is announced in the east, above the tight chain of the highest mountains that preclude the city of God to the human eye.

While they mock that which they don't see, they caress the sheep to be slaughtered, and the fat to be peeled, they seek monetary paper and paradise in slums between which the rooster repeats his song, Dawn becomes Aurora. The world awakens to the light and leaves behind the Owls, masters of the Long night, in the dens to devour the corpse of the great lie that nursed them in the eve.

To those who believe, to those who love, to those who hope to find the true meaning of my word, let this be your law.[25]

---

[25] Giuliano Kremmerz, *il Mondo Secreto*, Edizioni Rebis.

Giuliano Kremmerz - Opera Omnia

1.	Il Mondo Segreto	The Secret World (journal)	1896-1899
2.	Angeli e Demoni dell'Amore	Angels and Demons of Love	1898
3.	La Medicina Ermetica	On Hermetic Medicine	1900
4.	Il Libro degli Arcani Maggiori	A Treatise On the Major Arcana	1909
5.	La Porta Ermetica	The Hermetic Door	1910
6.	Commentarium	Commentaries (journal)	1910-11
7.	Lunazioni – Annotazioni sulle influence siiderali e lunari sulle piante I medicamenti le infermita del corpo umano	Lunations - Annotations on the sidereal and lunar influences on plants, medicines and infirmities of the human body	1913
8.	La Magia Divinatoria. I Tarocchi	Divinatory Magic, The Tarot	1921
9.	Conversazioni - Circolo Virgiliano,	Conversations at the Virgilian Circle	1921
10.	Conversazioni - Accademia Pitagora	Conversations at the Pythagoras Academy	1921
11.	Medicina Dei	Divine Medicine	1923
12.	La Morte	On Death	1923
13.	Dialoghi sull'Ermetismo	Dialogues on Hermeticism	1931
Manuscripts – Reserved for Members of the Myriam			
14.	Fascicola A – La Pragmatica Fondamentale **	Dossier A – The Fundamental Practice	
15.	Fascicolo B - I Preliminary di Pace **	Dossier B - The Preliminaries of Peace	
16.	Fascicolo C - Rito Individuale **	Dossier C - The Individual Rite	
17.	Fascicolo D - Il Primo Contatto **	Dossier D - The First Contact	
18.	Corpus Philosophicum Totius Magiae Restitutum**	The Complete Body of Philosophical Magic Restored	

part
FOUR

figure 11 – Julius Evola

CONTEMPORARY INITIATORY GROUPS

Julius Evola and the UR Group

Heroism is an *ascesis* in the strictest meaning of the word, and the hero is a nature so purified from the "human" element, as far as he is in ascesis: he participates in the same character of purity as the principle he embodies – Julius Evola.[1]

Along with the Myriam, the most influential initiatic circle operating in Italy, over the course of the last century was the UR Group. Founded in late 1926 and led by Julius Evola (1898-1974), a young philosopher, painter, poet, and artist along with Arturo Reghini (1878–1946) an erudite scholar noted for a scientifically rigorous approach to spiritualism as well as a leading exponent of Freemasonry and Pythagoreanism. In 1911, Reghini was initiated into a mysterious Pythagorean circle known as the "Schola Italica" by the musicologist Amadeo Armentano. The Schola Italica, claimed to be a continuation of a lineage that descended from an initiatory sodality based in Florence during the Renaissance and known as the Fratres Lucis.[2] In the mid-1920s, Reghini

---

[1] Julius Evola, essays from the journal La Vita Italiana.

[2] Italian historian Gaetano LoMonaco challenges the assertion of an

edited two journals, *Atanor* and *Ignis*, that prefigured the writings of the *UR* journal on initiatic studies and the meta-political issues facing Italy and the Occident. Reghini promulgated the revival of an ancient Roman inspired imperialism by extolling in numerous articles and public speaking engagements, the central role to be played by Italy, in heralding a new Occidental Renaissance. In an attempt to stir up public interest and influence the fledgling Fascist government, Reghini re-published in *Atanor*, his 1924 article on "Pagan imperialism", which was published on the eve of World War I as a clarion call to revive Roman—and hence Italian—imperialism. A response was quick to arrive from the Fascist journal *Gerarchia* (*Hierarchy*) by an anonymous writer using the pseudonym, Fermi (allegedly, Benito Mussolini). A series of contesting articles were exchanged back and forth between Reghini and Fermi, where Fermi questioned Reghini's assertion that Freemasonry could provide the requisite elite for a new Italy and recommended the best means for Reghini and his circle of Imperialists to influence the course of Italian society was by founding an academy, like those that guided princes and condottieri throughout the Renaissance. The most notable examples are Pomponio Leto's Roman Academy and Ficino's Platonic Academy.[3]

---

uninterrupted chain in the following terms: "Furthermore, when we talk about Schola Italica and the unbroken Italic-Roman tradition in relation to the current advocated by Armentano and Reghini, we must go there with feet of lead because all that glitters is not gold (in the sense that the claim of the Florentine mathematician and the Cosentine musician of being the exponents of an ancient pagan initiatory vein is anything but founded, indeed we could say that it is mendacious. In any case it is better not to say too much, it is better to assume a dubious attitude in this respect".

[3] *ATANOR rivista di studi iniziatici*, IGNIS rivista mensile di studi iniziatici, Case Editrice Atanor.

> Julius Evola told me that death is the continuation of life, the sublimation of (our self) history. He told me that from this one certain event—death—we can, we must draw, one by one the reasons for life. – Benito Mussolini (Taccuini Mussolini)

The UR Group was formed in the wake of the social conflicts arising after WWI and the Fascist March on Rome, in a period marked by intense forces acting simultaneously on physical as well as metaphysical levels. This turbulent backdrop fueled notions across Italy and Europe of an imminent "Decline of the West" and the stagnation of Western man. Concurrently, there began to emerge, throughout Italy and elsewhere in Europe, groups prepared to resist the course of this destiny by attempting to reorient society towards a return to origins and a resurgence of a "New Order" and a "New Man". The leaders of the UR sodality sought to influence the nascent Fascist movement by providing the body politic with a Roman and Olympian soul to support the formation of a new man (*l'uomo nuovo*). A new man rooted in an adamantine soul, spiritual in nature, yet who affirmed himself in heroic actions. Evola would characterize this new man as an Absolute Individual, detached from profane influences, self-sufficient like an autarchic Stoic of ancient Roman mold.[4]

The first issues from the journal *UR* were published on a monthly basis in 1927 and devoted to the study of philosophical and spiritualistic themes with contributions from a wide variety of qualified esotericists:

> The collaborators adopted the principle of anonymity, all of whom signed with a pseudonym because—as

---
[4] Julius Evola, *Teoria e Fenomenologia dell'Individuo Assoluto*, Edizioni Mediterranee.

stated in the introduction—the individual person counts for little, what they have to say of value is not of their creation or contrivance but reflects super-individual teachings and objectives.[5]

The UR group consisted of leading lights from a wide cross-section of Italian esoteric currents, including magists from the Kremmerzian school (Abraxa, Primo Sole, Nilius, Ekatlos), Pythagoreans from the Schola Italica (Pietro Negri, Luce, Saggittario) proponents of a Dantean vision of synthesizing the eagle with the cross (Havismat, Gic, Siro, Sirius), followers of Rudolf Steiner's teachings (Leo, Breno, Oso, Taurulus), and united under a Roman Imperialist banner.

The UR Group were positioned as agents of change that sought to influence the prevailing forces of society individually, culturally, and politically, by awakening a higher force to act, through its teachings and magical practices, on the general environment. Centered in Rome but with branches in other Italian cities, the UR Group formed, under the guidance of Reghini and Evola, a magical chain to cultivate forces and affect change (See Volume II for instructions on establishing a Magical Chain).[6]

Since the Risorgimento, initiates and their associated groups, have engaged through the agencies of esoteric practices to act magically and direct Italian leaders towards a spiritual and political renaissance. At the core of this ambitious project was the formation of a spiritual elite to lead the state. The creation of this aristocracy of the spirit, was the cornerstone of traditionalist thought, as well as an indispensable factor for the implementation

---

[5] Julius Evola, *Il Cammino del Cinabro*, Edizioni Mediterranee.

[6] *KRUR*, rivista di scienze esoteriche, n.12.

of an imperial plan. Because the "Ur Group", articulated a focused program, it was openly promulgated.[7]

Leo writes:

The first step of this initiatic journey involves a profound transformation and metamorphosis of oneself: All the exercises of inter-authoritative development will be paralyzed if the shell-limits that form the daily habits of man is not broken and even with that even a habitual pattern persists in the human subconscious.[8]

Perhaps the article that best summarizes the UR Group's *weltanschauung* or vision of life is EA's (Evola) contribution in Volume one "On the Magical View of Life". The article captures the major themes that permeate Evola's work, up to this point and by extension of the UR Group. The magical view of life articulates a doctrine of self-liberation, freedom from contingencies, both external and internal, a purification of the soul, with emphasis on a solar path of action as characterized by the warrior/kshatriya and the associated techniques of the Royal Art. In summary, a life anchored in an ascesis and self-transcendence with a heroic relationship to the world.

These are "truths" to be assumed in a given phase of the development, in view of a preliminary liberation and purification of the soul. Such a development may take this form especially in the "way of the warrior" – the kshatriya, to use the Hindu term. Once the fruit of such a discipline has been achieved, various

---

[7] Fabrizio Giorgio, *Roma Renovata Resurgat il tradizionalismo Romano tra Ottocento e Novecento* – Volume 2.

[8] *Introduzione alla Magia,* quale scienza dell'io, Volume 2, Edizioni Mediterranee.

perspectives may change and the point of view proper to the true transcendent realization should be accessed.

Self-overcoming, aside from being the object of rituals, is connected to a renewed, heroicized perception of the world and of life, not as an abstract concept of the mind, but as something that pulsates in the rhythm of one's own blood. It is the sensation of the world as power, or the sensation of the world as a sacrificial act. A greater freedom, with action as the sole law. Everywhere beings made of strength, and, at the same time, a cosmic breathing, a sense of height, of airiness.

Action needs to be liberated. It must be realized in and of itself, disinfected from mental fever, cleansed from hatred and craving. These truths must penetrate the soul: there is no place to go to, nothing to ask for, nothing to hope for, nothing to fear.[9]

Of the individual contributors to the UR and Krur journals, special attention should be placed on the writings that went under the pseudonym Abraxa, and with whom we've come to know as Ercole Quadrelli.[10] Other than Evola, Quadrelli's contributions are one of the few that are included in all three years of UR and Krur's existence. Ercole Quadrelli was a follower of the magist Giuliano Kremmerz and member of the Roman branch of the Myriam, Virgilian Circle. However, not much is known of him, other than the fact that he translated the influential late Renaissance Hermetical treatise: *Chymica Vannus-Commentatio de pharmaco catholico* (1666) by Johannes de

---

[9] *Introduzione alla Magia, quale scienza dell'io*, Volume 1, Edizioni Mediterranee.

[10] *Quaderni del Gruppo di Ur*, XVII IL Gruppo Di Ur.

Monte-Snyder, and wrote several illuminating articles and reviews on Hermeticism including "The Fedeli d'Amore" and "The Magic of Henry Cornelius Agrippa".

The presence of many articles by Abraxa, suggests the importance that the Kremmerzian influence held over the initiatic material published in the *Ur* and *Krur* journals. A close relationship was established with Evola, whereby Quadrelli would send his contributions to Evola for editing and refinement before their subsequent publication. The Abraxa articles were by far the most significant interventions on operative magical techniques and, as such, represent the heart of the UR Group's teachings.

SUMMARY OF ARTICLES BY ABRAXA IN UR & KRUR

UR Volume 1 (1927)	*UR* Volume 2 (1928)	*KRUR* (1929)
Knowledge of the Waters	Magic of the Ritual	The Cloud and the Stone
The Three Ways	Rhythms, Liberations, & Solutions	Communications
The Hermetic Caduceus and the Mirror	The Magic of Creation	The Magic of Victory
Instructions on "Breathwork"	Magical Unions	Knowledge of Sacrificial Action
Preparation According to the Hermetic Caduceus		
The Magical Operations on Two Vessels – Doubling		
The Magic of Images		

At the end of the second year of *UR* (1928), the mounting tensions, both existential and otherwise, began to take its toll over some of the Group's leaders and crescendoed into new heights that spilled over into a quarrel that split the members into two. One side supporting Reghini and Parise and the other Evola. This rupture terminated the working relationship between Reghini and Evola, over allegations that Evola plagiarized one of Reghini's most celebrated articles "Pagan Imperialism", using the name of the celebrated article for the title of Evola's book released later that year. As a result, the Evola-Reghini-Parise leadership team was dissolved, and in the third year, the journal underwent a change and a new name – *Krur*, with Evola assuming sole leadership responsibilities.

One of the specialized areas of research that the journal focused on was the collective roots of an authentic Hyperborean and Western tradition. Concurrently there appeared several articles throughout the UR monographs on the origins or collective roots of the Western tradition: On the Occidental Tradition, Hyperboria, and most notably an article attributed to a mysterious member named Ekatlos: "The Great ORMA: In Front and Behind the Scenes (La Grande Orma: La scena e le quinte)".

In 1929, the magazine *Krur* published an article "The Great Ora (acronym for Roma), in Front and Behind the Scenes" by an anonymous contributor who informs the readers of an auspicious event that occurred before the war (WWI), involving a ritual undertaken by a circle of initiates to revive the spiritual forces of Eternal Rome and herald victory of the Italian army in the great war to restore the "sacred homeland". A few years after this ritual took place, the same initiates made an offering to Mussolini—who became in 1922 Head of Government— of an ancient Etruscan lictorian *fasces*. Most of those who have dealt with this story indicate the mysterious contributor named "Ekatlos" was in fact Leone Caetani, Prince of Teano and Duke of Sermoneta, who, however, at the time of the publication of this article in *Krur*, was already living in Canada in voluntary exile from Italy. The various essayists and scholars who have written on this story also seem to agree that the word "Ekatlos" was due to an oversight by Evola, director of *Krur* who, by mistake, added an "s" to the osco-sabine word "EKATLO" whose translation into Italian is "ARALDO" (Herald).

Actually, in various ancient Roman and pre-Roman inscriptions the term EKATLO LARTIO can be found translated as "Herald" or "Hero". In reality, in the ancient Ausonic language EK-ATLO stands for "DA ATLI" or coming from the Ancient Saturnia Tellus ATLI (or ATLA), primitive seat of the mythical Atlanteans. We know from the learned studies of Camillo Ravioli and Reguzzoni, that the primitive Italic continent, which had the shape of an oak leaf, also incorporated Sardinia and Sicily as the Tyrrhenian sea did not exist and had a continuity that went from the Alps to the coasts of North Africa. The idea of creating a Group that was working ritually in the Italic-Roman Tradition, and reviving the Ancient Italic cults, came to Giustiniano Lebano, Supreme Pontiff of the Egyptian Order, under the inspiration of Ersilia Caetani Lovatelli, academician of the Accademia dei Lincei, an erudite scholar of antiquity, animator of several esoteric circles of the Capital, and Aunt to the aforementioned Leone Caetani.

> The two Rituals were carried out: one on 25 December 1913 in the Urbe's subsoil, the other on the Palatine Hill on 21 April 1914: both rituals were preceded by a demanding individual preparation from each of the Group members, according to the ascesis solemnly imposed by the Egyptian-Italian tradition to which we do not have to say more. The rituals carried out

produced a series of favorable events: the entry into the war of Italy, the victory that completed the unification of Italy with Trento, Trieste, Fiume, and the Dalmatian coast finally becoming reunited with the motherland and, shortly thereafter, the Fascist revolution.

This seemed to be the long-awaited definitive resurrection of Italy, with Mussolini in the form of the Dantean Veltro, re-instating the Imperium. But pressures from bourgeois, materialistic, and Catholic forces and the persistence of the narrow mindset of the "Italietta umbertina" (Little Italy of King Umberto) in many of the leading exponents of Fascism, led to the rapprochement with the Catholic Church, to the concordat, and finally to the persecution of all the inspired "pagans" of Italy. The law against secret societies did the rest, given that eight out of ten members of the EKATLO group were Freemasons! It was the former mayor of Naples and Senator of the Kingdom, Pasquale del Pezzo who delivered to Evola, through Vincenzo Gigante, the article "La Grande Orma": this was done in accordance with the instructions given by Don Leone Caetani before his departure to Canada. Gigante handed to Evola some typed sheets: at the top was a pencil note: "EK-ATLO" with a s placed in brackets, which indicated the secrecy of the document, or the circumspection with which Gigante had delivered the article. Evola thought that the "s" indicated a possible plural diphthong and the article written by EKATLOS was delivered to the printers. Years later Gigante clarified the story to Evola, pointing out the error and taking responsibility for not having explained better to the director of *KRUR* the meaning of the "aforementioned added s."

EKATLOS – THE "GREAT ORMA"; IN FRONT & BEHIND THE
SCENES

Today, work is being undertaken on a glorious monument, in whose central alcove will be placed a statue of archaic Rome. May this symbol revive, again, in all its power! Its light and splendor.

On a meandering street, centrally located, of the old Urbe, there is a strange little building, where at the time of the Caesars, the cult of Isis was practiced (with remnants of Egyptian obelisks). In the most recondite part of the building is placed, and still remains, a sign, that in certain terms refers to a resurgent Roman fortune, the Phoenix – resurgent from the flames. Around the sign, there are placed the following letters:

R.R.R.
I.A.T.C.P.

In 1929, after a half-century breach, a treaty of reconciliation was signed between the Italian state and the Holy See that established a separate state of the Vatican and allowed for Catholicism to become the official state religion of Italy. This turn of events caused the pagan imperialists of the UR Group to reassess their tactics and strategize new avenues to pursue. However, it should be noted that Mussolini viewed these turn of events in another light.[11]

---

[11] Benito Mussolini, *Taccuini Mussolini, il mulino*. Mussolini on Evola and the Conciliation between Italy and the Holy See: "Contrary to what is generally thought, I was not annoyed by the position of Dr. Julius Evola a few months before the Conciliation against any modulation of peace between the Holy See and Italy. The attitude of Dr. Evola, moreover, does not directly regard the relations between Italy and the Holy See, but that which, in his opinion, will be, over the centuries, the irreconcilability between Roman tradition and Catholic tradition.

It was under these circumstances, that emphasis on detachment from the horizontal plain of direct action to pursue an inner vertical tangent was developed and articulated in Evola's work on the Royal Art, *The Hermetic Tradition*. To affect real change on the outside one must first realize change within. While in alchemical terms 'transformations' are changes that occur at the physical-chemical level (Saturn, Lunar) and 'transmutations' are those which occur at the psycho-mental plane (Mercury), true change occurs when the individual human state (humus, personality complex) is transcended and being is centered in the spiritual (Solar). Hence, making gold by the 'Royal Art' meant the process by which man's consciousness is raised to finer Solar states or enlightenment. This is also a reference to Dantean syllogisms: "incielare" and "inparadisare" allow for the intuition of first causes (essences) and a birds-eye perspective of the effects. As with the transmutation of 'base' substances to 'nobler' ones, occurring in the mineralogical domain, so to in the human context through the purification of psycho-physical vehicles. Man was said to have liberated his vital energy by merging with consciousness. Transcendence is fully realized by the grounding of being into the spiritual realm to cascade down and permeate through the four bodies as vehicles of light.[12]

Hence, having identified Fascism with the survival of the Roman tradition, nothing would remain to be seen as opposed to any view of the history of the unversalist order."

[12] Homayun Taba, *Alchemy and Yoga*, Bihar School. Alchemy is that system which liberates energy and expands consciousness. Consciousness expansion takes place by the removal of obstructing factors which yoga terms *kleshas* and alchemy calls dross. Afflictions viewed from the point of alchemy constitute those corrosive properties that rust the personality-complex. While in the alchemical sense "transmutations' are those changes which occur at the physico-chemical level, 'transformations' are those which are noticed at the

After the mixed results obtained from his experiences in the UR group and then later with directing the journal *La Torre* (*The Tower*), Evola set off to the mountain peaks of the Dolomites to envision a strategy aimed at a broader audience than the narrow Italian scope. What resulted was a further refinement of the Evolian vision, centered in Hermetic and heroic principles and articulated in some of his most arresting works – *The Hermetic Tradition, Revolt Against the Modern World, Mask and Faces of Contemporary Spiritualism, Mystery of the Grail,* and the *Doctrine of the Awakening.*

In the mid-thirties and right up to the war years, Evola would frequently visit Vienna as a guest of the conservative revolutionary writer Rafael Spann, son of the economist Othmar Spann. While based in Vienna, Evola enlarged his network of acquaintances and sympathizers to include a network of intellectuals sharing a similar Ghibelline vision of a trans-national Western Empire. In what appears as a *doppelganger* to his experience directing the UR Group, Evola set up a group or nucleus of individuals in Vienna, dedicated to metaphysical studies and known as the "*Kronidenbund*" or the "Circle of Kronos." Kronos (Chronos) the Greek god of ancient time, was equivalent to the Roman Saturn, the ruler of the Golden Age. Kronos, according to myth, was dethroned by Zeus, who threw him out of the chariot, exiling him to a desert island where he slumbers. Being immortal, Kronos cannot die: he sleeps wrapped in funerary linen, until the time of his awakening, where he will be reborn, not in the form of an old man, but as a child. His rebirth will coincide with the beginning of a new cycle. The Chronides are his followers, vowed to

psycho-spiritual plane. Alchemy is a science which transmutes the base metals into gold, and has to be understood in the light of this dual metamorphosis. Making gold by their 'art' meant the process by which man's consciousness would be raised to finer states of responsiveness.

prepare for his awakening. As the true god of origins and roots, his awakening and rebirth symbolizes the correct spiritual orientation of a "conservative revolution."[13]

In an article entitled 'The Guardian of the Threshold' (Il Guardiano della Soglia) Francesco Waldner writes:

> In the very first years after the war, on a trip from Vienna to Salzburg, I had a casual conversation with a traveler in my compartment, if I remember correctly, he was a doctor, the conversation fell, I do not know how, on metaphysical questions, and he told me that he often met in Vienna with a very advanced scholar who led a group that had a large following of admirers: "He is an Italian" he added, and I asked him who he was, and he replied his name is Julius Evola. I was very surprised.
>
> He told me that Evola became disabled as a result of an aerial bombing (during the war). He referred to his infirmity, however, as having in no way dimmed his full mental lucidity; he told me that his magnetism exercised a great power over the people who were part of the group; that he was a strong-willed man of great intellectual strength, who kept his love and his interest in life intact. Then my traveling companion concluded saying that even though he was an invalid, he was not, because he participated in all the senses of life, more so than himself.[14]

---

[13] *Quaderni del Gruppo di Ur*, XVII IL Gruppo Di Ur.
[14] A.A.V.V, *Testimonianze Su Evola*, Francesco Waldner, Edizioni Mediterranee.

DAVID PANTANO

Marco Daffi on the Andromeda Rite

Throughout the second half of the twentieth century, with the deaths of Kremmerz (1930), Reghini (1946), and with Evola physically disabled (whose world-view re-oriented towards existential problems of how men should remain standing amid the ruins), Marco Daffi became the leading light in Italy of esoteric and initiatic studies. He was an authoritative figure at the prestigious Accademia Tibertina of Rome, conducting numerous talks and engaging in private consultations with aspirants seeking knowledge of the Hermetic arts. Despite their divergent methodologies, Marco Daffi's influence extended to a young aspirant researching the practical application of Alchemical-Hermeticism by the name of Giammaria Gonella of Genova. There soon followed a regular correspondence and collaboration from the early 50s to the late 60s, which led to Giammaria revising Marco Daffi's letters and adding refinements to many of his published works on Alchemical-Hermeticism.

> When Marco Daffi invited me to work in his laboratory, he agreed, to record for future memory, notes gleaned from his oratory, with the authority to elaborate on them in one form or the other. In fact, Marco Daffi's writings are suited more for adepts than for novices, since only those who have dirtied their hands in the Work will be able to draw the right understanding from such recondite intuitions and inventions.

In operative terms, Daffi's essays explore the fringes of Hermetic discourse by addressing subjects as diverse as the appearance of reversed images in the astral plane, monadic entanglement, double syzygy, female initiation,

figure 13 - Marco Daffi

and spiritual avatars. Daffi's writings on female initiation, remains "*rara avis*" a rare event, barely mentioned in the vast literature covering Hermeticism and alchemy. In doctrinal terms, Daffi's texts are illuminating, due to their poignant observations on initiation, initiatory orders, astral entities, and on the fluidic current of creation. In summary, Marco Daffi's body of writings is an eloquent testimony to the continuity, timeliness, and innovation of the Alchemical-Hermetic tradition in Italy.[15]

GIAMMARIA ON "MARCO DAFFI AND HIS WORK"

In his own words, "one could say Morkohekdaph (Marco Daffi is the Italianized form) was inexistent ... because he was an abstract entity from an invisible world; belonging to the realm of visions, of magic, of reincarnations, to the world that clings to the subterranean fields of the subconscious and does not form part of the physical person."

I found myself in the galaxy of Andromeda advancing towards the Pleiades (in relative terms: Pleiades = Sky or astral realm, Andromeda = Earth or spiritual manifestation) on a mission to what I, not knowing my real name, shall conventionally call Galaxy of the Dense Planet. It was necessary, therefore, to cross an electrified barrier of Black Archons, and for this reason I had to disassemble myself like components of a machine that could be dismantled into pieces and pass through a sieve, without disintegrating. I remained "entangled", for reasons that I shall omit, of my "3rd piece" or intermediate body, and with this lost contact with my other pieces, that is my: Feminine (self), male Eon, female Eon, thus remaining devoid

---

[15] Giammaria, *Marco Daffi e la sua Opera*, Editrice Kemi.

of a NORMAL fluidic body. However, as an advanced initiate, with the power to remake and readjust my "immortal" self at will. I remade myself with (black) infernal feminine components, with a pseudo intermediate body, into an incomplete Avatar that doesn't function properly. The problem I faced was how to recall my true intermediate body, how to expel this fictitious and incomplete one and to return to my original, pure and integral state of Andromeda: and resume contacts with the people of my lineage.

On earth I witnessed two eras: an Atlantean, where I lived in a sweet slumber... and an Egyptian-Phoenician-Chaldean era, that superimposed over my previous constitution with the solar initiation of a Chaldean Master. No one knew of my true past not even the Egyptian-Chaldean Order, to which I was affiliated with. Forgetful though I was then (I remember it now), I was driven by a desire to return to my true self. But since the problem was not to build a second Wood of Life (lifeline), rather to expunge it, the forms of initiation that were made available to me: the Egyptian-Chaldean, as well as the recent Neapolitan (18th century), could only result in failure.

I have memories of displacements, either as a typical Avatar (for example, passing through a predisposed body, analogous to the ejection of a Magister, as an entity not already animated, but Void, in the saturnian-lunar shell) and as a being of the numinal world of Andromeda, to which passing from one body into another is not a problem, but simply the coordination of my physical body. I've come to understand this constitution as having been the source of all my inadequacies and errors possible, from Egypt to Naples, to today. This twilight manifestation of myself led inevitably to my oblivion, not only, but extremely important to note, to remake myself but also to see the problems only through the most external aspect, in a positive sense. There are two factors, however, that have escaped me: one concerns my debilitating psycho-physical conditions, the other of my expansiveness. Kremmerz assumed it was a simple characterological anomaly, while, in reality it was a structural problem that he had completely ignored.

The problem was actually twofold:

1) To come to terms with the fact that nothing could be effectively changed.

2) Not to construct or reconstruct a Second Wood of Life (lifeline), but to delete those conditions that have been profoundly buried, that is my original self from the Andromeda-Pleiades.

Even before we met, Kremmerz had intuited in one of his letters that there were two "Judges" that symbolized problems, one was my weak psycho-physical condition, the other remained unknown to him, but simply speculated. Perhaps he believed that in this life - I had only to solve the Egyptian problem ... and that the other problem – mysteriously unknown, would have to be resolved later; I did not know, only that, by releasing me in such a way, I had deformed and altered the problem, which even Kremmerz caught a glimpsed of, in 1926, shortly before I knew it and reduced everything to an arrangement with a "Canadian" Egyptian order, that I came into contact with later on.

In December of 1929, (the date of our last meeting) Kremmerz had a final insight with respect to the essence of my being. He wrote "I applaud your intuition on discovering that you are an incomplete Avatar and for remembering to search for your magical companion, after distant aeons and cosmic spaces, and this is also an insight into the faraway origins of the human species". But he did not see that I wanted, even desperately, in a semi-conscious way to say that I was incomplete and that not even temporary relationships let's call them volatile, the result of a struggle, I maintained, until the "incomplete" avataric state (expression that refers to an inability to synthesize upstream, the superimposition of three solar initiations, under the subordination of the main one) was resolved.

My work was an impulse, without the memory of the Electric Barrier that anchored my teachings, that is the reverse of Kremmerz's intuition, of having to resume relations with the Canadian Egyptian Order, which instead, I had now detached myself from. The problem lies in a work of expurgation, carried out between 1956 and 1961, in a mental and philosophical rectification, despite the impediments arising from the negative forces from my impurities, from the contingent constraints, and from the lack of a truly integrated fluidic body.

However, shocking these words may appear if understood solely under a linear and horizontal trajectory of history and not, beyond the veil of these strange verses, under the regularized order of depth. In a paradigmatic sense, the name: MORKOHEKDAPH should be seen as the coagulation of a constellation of ideas, strongly emotive, crafted, from a cohesive impulse derived from memory, in an autonomous system, from a representation that is proposed today as if it were yesterday, and to be developed further tomorrow. Of Marco Daffi's "tomorrow" who can say, for it is a death and an irreversible outcome of death. Of his "yesterday" he said it himself, although in an ambiguous, obscure and, I'm not sure how consciously, fanciful manner. He wrote:

... today in the course of my natural life ... originally my task in this existence was personal, it was that of expiation, of rebalancing, and the more that it seems as not having been written by the Fates, that I should quickly liquidate the accretions layered on myself, accumulated in three successive avataric layers. However, the gesture of self-denying that the incarnation was received avatarically (from the Avatar) is not mine. It is worthy of a simple twist of Fate ... the physical manifestation, occurred in a period that initially was to rebalance the physical transformation, to face the profane. I first came into contact with Kremmerz, to stabilize a relationship, and to tap into the resurgent memory of his Egyptian past and to receive only the facts concerning my precise persona, which Kremmerz completely mistook, until it was corrected by my memory. I recollected that there were two stages of my transmutation and reconciliation with the confraternity of the Egyptian Order of Canada ... the said stages were two repairs.

The errors committed by Giuliano Kremmerz were many to which I have outlined in detail in two reports: one exhaustive and the other personal ... the fact of the matter is the repair was not successful and at some point ... I found myself stuck in a situation having to deal with a serious crisis, in a fearsome New Year's Eve of 1932, concerning the Pharaonic Group, with the attempt to repair my undefined fate. The first plan of action was to form seven numinal sections, corresponding to the seven forms of intelligence, and which then would naturally become disconnected from the human bond and take on an autonomous form. If not by karmic force and by my immaturity, the same immaturity that is characteristic of avatars, resulted in an unrestrained and indeterminate struggle against my adverse elements ... The struggle, lasted 21 years, and failed to realize the original program, however, it was worth making progress and giving rise to my oldest Atlantean atavism and consequently the most profound hieratic tendency.[16]

Giammaria and the Body of Peers

After the Second World War, the Myriam and the UR Group continued to exercise a strong influence on the doctrinal and operative trajectories of initiatory groups and single practitioners in contemporary Italy. With this backdrop, the Corpo dei Pari (we shall refer to them from now as the Corpo dei Pari rather than the Body of Peers which is a literal English translation) were formed in the early 1960s by Giammaria Gonella (1924-) and unlike their predecessors, the members adopted a loose, non-hierarchical and self-experimental organizational structure. Giammaria writes: "the so-called Corpo dei Pari was founded in Genova around 1960/1961 as a working group with the aim of giving back to Alchemy its rightful place as an "initiatory path" – to counteract

---

[16] Giammaria, Preface to *Dissertamina*, by Marco Daffi, Edizioni Alkaest.

figure 14 - Marco Daffi & Giammaria

the dominant influence of Magical-Hermeticism, and correct the popular belief that Alchemy is a proto-chemistry." It is clear that Giammaria is referencing the residual effect of the disproportionate influence of

figure 15– Giammaria the Archer

the Myriam and the UR Group on the current hermetical scene, when he states, "to counteract the dominant influence of Magical-Hermeticism". At the very least, the Corpo dei Pari could be construed as a school of thought and of action operating under the guise of Alchemy, and where the vision of the world informs the idea (to be taken as a working hypothesis) that triggers an individual act of conscious Self illumination. This is, in fact, the Principle that becomes aware of the Self. To explain further, outside of any metaphor, the Alchemical world view sees the human being as a spatial and temporary individuation, which takes shape in an historic and biographic context, that is only apparent to itself as a separate entity from all others: whereas the person (mask) is the manifestation of a single energetic field, that in itself is undefinable and indescribable, in act (*Telesma*).

The basic practices of the Corpo dei Pari revolved around a process of reintegration of the self into the Self leading to transfiguration into Being (Numen). Alchemy in this sense referred to the process of becoming Mercury, that is permeating all things from within. Giammaria wrote: "It is difficult to explain what Alchemy is by remaining on the outside, writing of it can only illustrate the components and explain the operating methods, and articulate the story, but all the words used would not suffice to translate only one realized experience: Mercury remains forever bound to Proteus."

figure 16– Giammaria, Icarus

Giammaria's writing on Hermeticism is useful to those seeking to disentangle the many "secrets" hidden in the language of Tradition. The symbol, understood with the appropriate keys, can reveal that which Alchemical wisdom has hidden behind aphorisms, cryptograms, and ciphers. They are the considerations of a man who has learned to observe the world and its events with disenchanted eyes. The material becomes an "historical" artifact through which one can follow the inner path of the author who reveals, through his work, the most important stages of his personal iteration of Consciousness. The texts include seemingly incongruous themes, demonstrating how fluid and amorphous Mercury is in everything and everywhere. This is how the author expresses his own Being, how he transmits the Fire and manifests what has been revealed to him by the heavens, once again demonstrating that Hermes is "concealed" in the texts and is useful to those who are prepared to "dirty their hands". It is necessary to submerge and explain the process from the inside out. Alchemy is identified with the "act of doing" Alchemy. It becomes the only real dimension in which one lives and works, without limits, grafted onto the fabric of one's being. Work as Being. To quote Giammaria – "not by the brain alone, but through the heart will Alchemy become an intuition."

ON THE HUMAN CONDITION

The human being (whether male or female) is a spatial and temporal event that takes shape from the unified energy field that is the (universal and supernal) principle of manifestation. Each person is therefore a unique manifestation but is not separate from "others", just as a drop of water is not distinct in the ocean. The individual identifies with the person (mask) within a unique undefinable source that is beyond all terminology.

Typically, the individual "believes" he is separate from "others" and from the principle by which he fundamentally manifests and identifies with the "I", "You", "They", and "Them", unaware that the "others" are, like him, also a drop of water in the sea. And all are made of the same matter as water in the ocean. This mask covers all the creatures of the universe – where a sort of diffuse animation reigns.

Instead of identifying with their mask (person), with their physical and temporal identifications, if the individual were to dilate their consciousness and transfer awareness to that "which" lies beyond the biographical limits, the self would make the I (identity) fall on the Principle (from which the self is molded by the Self) and would realize the Great Hermetic Work. One could then perceive the universe as their own body and could live

Life (existence) as purely representative or as a dream of the unique mind in the personal mind...

Deciphering the complex symbolism of alchemy and pursuing a synthesis between different Western and Oriental traditions will lead to the development of a nucleus for a spiritual path suitable for modern times. The alchemical laboratory is located within the operator. All the representations and symbols are related to different states and realities of the Work (sulphur = spirit, mercury = soul, salt = body). Athanor is the man himself, while "metals" represent the individual psycho-physiological complexes. Fire is the psychic charge used in the Work, the awareness. The "dense" Lead represents one's own individuality, formed by complex psychic (psyche) fields; The "Subtle is constituted" by the Self, the Numen, the Deus Absconditus and is disaggregated from the historical self, the point of contact between identification of the personal and the "individuating transpersonal" self. By this process, Lead will be transformed into Gold, that is, individuation of the historical-bound individual will merge with the archetypal consciousness of the Principle. The fundamental concept, both of the Work and of Life itself, is precisely that of the Principle of things, which is a unified field of energy placed beyond the Time-Space paradigm, and beyond the dualism of energy and matter. This is the universal mind, God, Great Spirit, Abstract, Great Magical Agent, indefinable, and unknowable. It is the Void that manifests through the Universe, with universal laws, and is the substance of all structures. It is in the being of humans that the Principle expresses itself in its fullness, becoming intelligent in the form of consciousness.

Alchemical-Hermeticism is the preferred term used by the Pari. Alchemy is a branch of Hermeticism which includes magic, astrology, cabbala, and divination.

Giammaria describes alchemy as the transposition of consciousness from the historically-bound personalized individual to the archetypal trans-personalized Self.[17]

We are all traveling, on a journey of which we only know the date of departure but not that of arrival, let alone the destination, neither the duration, nor the meaning .... This being the case, we are badly prepared as travelers. Can we compensate for this ignorance: or assume that traveling is an unique opportunity to face the issue in its complexity, not in the certainty of resolving the problems, but in the hope "of a positive outcome", or an alternative, above all, that does not lack aesthetic value.

This is the choice (but is it really a choice?) of the alchemist (also called *artifex* or *opifex*) who is considered a pilgrim, a traveler, searching for a destination which in reality is to be found within. Be that as it may, it's a working hypothesis, in the logic of an itinerary and a destination that has to be "invented"; so that the future includes all that will be created. Consenting to an orientation of this kind, in the 1960s, the Pari (Peers) worked on constructing a reliable map of the path. They had very little to use as a starting point and material of dubious value that needed to be validated by the Regent of the Corpo. They were engaged in a program of partial anastylosis (restoration) of the Alchemical-Hermetic doctrine, its variegated facets, and its reformulation. The problem arose from the difficulty of accessing an authentic "alchemical path", to use as an initiatory model. In other words, it was a problem of direct transmission. After two centuries (at least since the eighteenth century) of silence on the subject, disinformation, lack of authentic "testimonials" or direct communications by operators ("*auctores*") of the operations, there was an absence of authentic details. The problem is—as usual—one of language. In the same way

---

[17] Giammaria, *Gli Excerpta*, Editrice Kemi.

that clothes wear out and distort over time, so to do the symbols (the archetypal clothing) which constitute the Alchemical-Hermetic language wear out and gradually change meaning, with certain symbols eventually becoming obsolete.

In any case, this is how the Corpo dei Pari, as a group, were formed. It was from the heart that they turned their thoughts to those who had worked to revive or adapt a doctrinal patrimony. Their work and collaboration resulted in the publication of both major and minor texts on Alchemical-Hermeticism. The Pari were publicly ignored, as if they were mute (and in a certain sense they were) and exploited as well, but not for personal or worldly objectives. They did not take advantage of their findings, rather they had opportunities to touch "moments of the summit" as a follow-up to their *Iter*, by gaining knowledge of their actions. If they instead, behaved like "*traditores*" (translators or traitors), for the very reason that they had transferred their knowledge to everyday purposes, then it would be worthwhile to say, thank you for what they gave.

It is easy to understand the importance of work from an "*equipe*", if we consider that since the 1700s Europe has been missing alchemists of a masterful calibre. Meanwhile, the fashion for "esoteric societies" had taken off, which has nothing to do with the Great Work of Alchemy, and takes place under the banner of "alone, you will be all yours" (*si solo, sarai tutto tuo*).

Within "esoteric societies" and the so-called "initiatic orders", there began a discourse on magic other than the traditional one, which is another operative species of Hermeticism. The Neapolitan Enlightenment (of the seventeenth century) propagated a form of magic which has been called "Egyptian" and which has come to constitute the leitmotif of the magical current in

Southern Italy. Emerging from this Masonic seminary are the names of Raimondo di Sangro, Prince of San Severo, Cagliostro, the Knight d'Aquino, as well as the techniques known as Arcana Arcanorum or "high degrees of the ladder of Naples". In the theurgical itinerary there is the construction a Body of Glory for alchemical "terminology", since the Body of Glory, in alchemy, is a body that survives and that requires an "absolutely other" operative process, another "iter".

The magical practice that goes under the name "Egyptian" or Scala di Napoli, has therefore taken inspiration in the "de quo" environment that took place in the nineteenth century field of Freemasonry especially with the fringe groups of Freemasonry, which involved figures such as Bocchini, Lebano, De Servis, Caetani (Ottaviano), Kremmerz, and—in the twentieth century—with others who saw themselves as heirs to the *Secretum Secretorum* of "Osidirean" ancestry. On the fringe of this current was Marco Daffi, who, due to his isolation, fortunately was able to concentrate on alchemical studies without distraction. For the record, it is worth noting that the rituals of the Scala di Napoli are manifestly of a Gnostic matrix and of an "antinomian" type (see the Nicolaiti, Fibonites – Simon and Capocrate).

Much of what has been written on the Corpo dei Pari is incorrect, especially by exponents of that undergrowth (peppered with professorial titles) that protrudes out from fermented fields. There was no true affiliation with any Kremmerzian and/or post-Kremmerzian environment on the part of the Peers, and not even by Daffi, and the Corpo was absolutely autonomous and extraneous from them. On the other hand, in "*stricto sensu*", Daffi was never an alchemist, and even less was Kremmerz a magist, yet these ideas provided the opportunity to rediscover alchemy, which in the first half of the twentieth century, as an initiatory path in Italy (and Europe as well), was virtually extinct. There is no lack, even before the eighteenth and nineteenth centuries, of popular books and essays, written by "*auditores*" (scholars, rarely "cultivators") but not by an operator "*auctores*" ... in other words it is a series of "dead ends."

Therefore, in terms of an acculturation, Kremmerz and above all Daffi, although rooted in the eighteenth century magical-ceremonial vein, could have triggered a "*rentree*" on the Italian scene, at least by Alchemical-Hermeticism. The Corpo dei Pari should not be mistaken as an esoteric society or an initiatory order, as one might think from the tone and tenor of the *Proclamations* and subsequent publications.[18] Rather they should be understood in the spirit of *"epater le bourgeois"*. In fact, there are no proclamations that elicit "the awakening of a higher force, to be used as an aid to individual work"[19] or any component "of that species of the psychic body that one wills to create, by evoking a real influence from above so that the possibility of practicing behind the scenes even on socio-political forces" remains.

However, this program of ideas, that goes under the qualification of "Egyptian Order", has nothing of an Alchemical-Hermetic provenance. For his time, Marco Daffi was the only exponent of Alchemical-Hermeticism, and none of his initiatives were intended to assume a resumption of cultural activities. It was the Corpo dei Pari that came to compensate for this emptiness, with the intention—in the first instance—of setting up a working group in order to compose and collect testimonies in an

---

[18] See the article by David Pantano on the Corpo dei Pari, "The Return of Hermes."

[19] Reference to Evola's preface of "Introduction to Magic" by the UR Group.

organic and modern form of Alchemical Hermeticism and—secondly—to provide an opportunity for the Peers to be more than "*lectores*" themselves. The facts are:

1. the Corpo could not have been constituted; that it was, is based on a decision to launch a challenge to oneself to succeed in revitalization of oneself and total resonance with the alchemical path;

2. given that at the time of the foundation, the scope of the preparation of the human 'material' to execute the "first field of action" means it could not be administered "*ad hoc*" ....

To put it in words of those who have lived or still experience that reality ... the Corpo does not assume either physical or juridical forms, rather it is an imaginary entity, which coagulates around a name, according to the principles of magic, by which the members are called Pari (Peers). To organically rectify any misunderstanding, the different functions performed by the members, at various times and occasions, emphasize the potential capacity of each person to realize the various levels of the Work.

Let each person consider himself an autonomous individual and then the cement of the Corpo can be seen as the idea which they adhered to. The words of another Pari say this well: "The Corpo is basically the sounding board for the Voice." Another member states that: "Each Peer is an actor with respect to the others, so that it follows that inside the Corpo dei Pari lives and plays a drama, a tragedy, a comedy and sometimes even a farce." One representation even takes form as a musical complex: "... there is the "all", when all the Peers (as soloists of the "ensemble") interact, more or less harmoniously and in time with the counterpoint, during the concert and especially at the ending, when the soloist must be able to perform the melody of his own vocation."

A "*soror*" (female initiate) can be found in the figurative arts, and to delineate this metaphor further, painters and sculptors approach "(alchemical) work in an analogous manner to exercising an errand", where individuals dotted with so-called charisma have no bearing with respect to their consecration as an "artist." And others say: "Herein lies the strength of the Corpo dei Pari, by maximizing the archetypal aspects of Hermes with the acquaintance of friends, without the filter of rituals or the conditioning of intermediaries." Also: "The others are the images of our qualities and our reactions, we see what we seek and what we love: coming forth in this dream is a violence to one's personal biography, incomplete we unify with those other aspects that, united, can participate in the realization of the common project". And others again state that: "... if we see the Corpo (Body) as a stream of thoughts, it is not permissible for there not to be a common line of action, even if the formalization of the Work must necessarily take on personal clothing and colors."

This heterogeneity (of members) is not to be seen as a freedom of style but as a qualitatively different instance. It's a fact that "the different approaches to the same subject, on the part of the different Peers" gave life and dynamism to the Corpo, which on the other hand acts as a sounding board "from a wider field of reflection and speculation" as an "instrument built with art and not left to chance" as one observes. In the words of another:

> ... in the Corpo (Body) everyone is seen a window to the depths of the existential problematic, in their own way, even in the analogous perspective of entering "orchards of the inner Sun", a perspective that unites the Pari (Peers), as the common denominator in the

"search", which anyway, each member has to discover themselves as an exponential numerator, that is both: composite and prime within themselves and of themselves.

In the Corpo, there never was any form of proselytism, the discourse was always discreet, if not secret. And it was never an "order," or an "academy," neither a "church", or "a confraternity," or an "*huis generis*" association. Instead as admonished by the Regent, the Corpo dei Pari can be summarized as follows:

> The Corpo dei Pari is like a banquet, where the Regent sits at the head of the table.
> Moderation is a function of the convivial discipline.
> All are guests, in all respects,
> Like with books to take or to leave,
> to fast or taste whatever and how much one likes,
> to pass food, to converse or to abstain,
> The Corpo dei Pari is not a license for merit,
> if it were it would no longer be itself,
> for it is strictly forbidden to whomsoever even tries
> to corrupt the body into an "order".

Therefore, the reader is left with little or no knowledge or of what alchemy is. For those fortunate to read these lines, the operations of alchemy occur in the "vision" of an alchemical principle called Mercury, and in religious terminology God – spiritually know as the Great Spirit, Hermetically as the One, and scientifically as the Void (also the Unified Field of Forces), and so on. It is, and they are:

1. undefinable, ineffable, undifferentiated, *per se* they are empty of everything, but full of every possibility by which the universal manifestation is reflected, in their objectification ... in their sensorialization;

2. in tension to realize the knowledge of themselves by means and through the World, its objectifications, and its clothing. Nature, on the other hand, is known by its true face by observing its reflection in a mirror, becoming aware of itself as an object ...

3. reflected in Man as the spearhead in the process of awareness;

4. the Great Work of Alchemy and of the processes (iter) that the alchemical operator must come to terms with at the end of his quest for knowledge (in order to internalize the information) of the One in All and the All in One.

Alchemical symbolism offers an "*ad hoc*" key to the visualization and interpretation along this initiatory path. The significance of the symbol (seen as an image par excellence) is profound, radical, and penetrates deeply into the psyche, it is beyond rationality, instincts, and sensations. The imaginal contains the "repository of depths" of the "cerebrum" (which is more than the brain commonly understood). In this respect, the human being is like a memory bank, reaching back to ancestral times, and acting as a "universal encyclopedia". Since the scope of Alchemical-Hermeticism tends to interest man in a global context, the key to identifying a suitable starting point—and its completion—are provided by images and Alchemical-Hermetic symbols. Now that the reader understands the "way of transmutation of lead into gold" they should know that along this path "their total awareness is required" to understand the Principles:

Therefore, be aware that:

1. The depth (meaning the Principle) of the mind is without end and therefore capable of infinite visions as projections.
2. The vision of the world; seen as a Non-I, should instead be understood as an Alter-Ego, that will make it vanish "as something other than the self", in the realization of the Great Work.[20]

---

[20] Giammaria, *Introduction to the da gli Atti degli Corpo dei Pari*, Edizioni Alkaest.

figure 17– Amor, the Roman Venus

O bountiful Venus, mother of the race of Aeneas, delight
of gods and men, who beneath the gliding constellations
of heaven, fillest with life the ship-bearing sea and
the fruit-producing earth; since by thy influence every kind of
living creature is conceived, and, springing forth, hails
the light of the sun.

- Lucretius (*On the Nature of Things*)

IN SUMMA

The Italic initiatic tradition, presented in this study, is rooted in a vision of life that is spiritual in nature and Hermetic in practice. The Hermetic *forma mentis* sees life as an all-encompassing and inter-connected whole by virtue of the original One (Principle). As the well-known phrase from the Emerald Tablet of Hermes suggests ("as it is above, so it is below"), there is an emanational continuity linking the macrocosm with the microcosm where everything is connected via a spiritual agency.

To draw from a broader range of references, the Hermetic practitioner privileges alternative modes of cognition such as thought-by-images, intuition, mnemonics, and dream states to develop an epistemological system, an *Hermetica Ratio* that derives the plurality of phenomena (vestiges) from their archetypal origins (Numen). By representing the WORLD, MAN, and the GREAT WORK, as images within a greater mandala of life, and clearly formulated into operational reference points, the Star of Hermes shines equally in the super-rational as well the rational spheres – and if rightly practiced, can magically evoke a Hermetic force for thinking, signifying, and acting.[21]

---

[21] Giammaria, *Da gli Atti degli Corpo dei Pari*, Edizioni Alkaest.

The fundamental practice is to experientially meditate on the impermanent nature of phenomena and especially one's own body and mind. Thus, the initiate comes to the profound recognition of the preciousness of their life and the time spent on the path to liberation.

The Golden Bough initiation outlined the Orphic, Pythagorean, and indigenous Italic traditions associated with a heroic style of life that is Olympian, as was characterized by the fire purifying rituals (Vesta) of the ancient Romans and Āryas. In Hermetic terms, the element of Water refers to the currents of love associated with the cultivation of will. Through the exercise of divine love—known under a variety of names as the path of Venus, amor, heroic furies, platonic ecstasy, or the state of Mag—the initiate cultivates a gnosis that opens a channel within the self, permitting entry into deeper levels of consciousness and higher realms of reality.

The Magic Door identified the initiatory practices to effect an alchemical inner transformation, with the goal of re-integrating being with the Numen or soul, to the extent that the initiate's *prima materia* becomes the *materia prima*. The element of Fire is dominant and refers to the luminous body of light associated with the faculties of visualization and intelligence. The *in-paradisare* or *in-cielare* referenced by Dante are realized states of *en-lighted-ness*.

The final section on the *Secret Fire of Azoth*, articulated the sidereal practices of the most important Italic initiatic circles to cultivate and sustain a Soul-centered being by attaining mastery over the fifth element of Aether, also known as Azoth, the Fixed Star of the Avataric state and associated with the liberation of consciousness from the physical envelope. A transpersonal state of being where consciousness fuses with vital energy and resides as pure awareness, known to the Vedic Āryas as the Atman and the Romans as Numen. By means of a laborious practice, involving the processes of solve et coagula, the adept realizes, if justice permits, a fully integrated and harmonious self (Numen) able to separate consciousness from the hyliac layer and project this cluster of consciousness (body of light) across the inner planes of reality, such as dreams and astral projections, and manifest it externally through auspicious events and synchronicities. As Dante references in the *Divine Comedy*, by resisting the forces of dissolution associated with the river Lethe (identification with hyliac and biographical data) the initiate drinks from the river of Euone where identification with the Numen is congealed, and projects outward to manifest through multiple levels of being.

Giammaria advises:

... there will awaken an inner Sun to affect a dis-identification of psychic contents, by means of a constant conscious observation that "distills" the contents until they become transparent. "Making the volatile fixed" means to solidify and stabilize the conscious experience of Life within the parameters of day-to-day self-hood (individuality). A possible interpretation of the symbol of the cross could be understood by the horizontal line representing the flow of material life bound through the space-time paradigm, and by the vertical line representing the unconditioned and infinite supernal life. An important exercise to "de-realize" from time and space, by breaking habitual engagements with existential situations. The only reality that counts at this point is to adjust the frame (how the Self relates with its periphery), in the background of an anonymous, trans-personalized, and timeless consciousness.[22]

The tell-tale sign of an adept that is fully centered at the core of his being, or Numen, are the projections of spiritual fire through an auric vibration manifested as inner light or radiating fragrances blossoming with archetypal perfumes. As a concept that transcends the *principium individuationis* by delving into the forces at the root of being, the concept of personal and subjective will is absent. But, Homer teaches us that power is transmitted from God to man. In the Greek concept of *Menos* we refer to a devouring force, a fire that takes possession of man as an expression of God. This altered state of consciousness, however, is obtainable through prayer, as seen in *Iliad* XVII, 210: "He that Ares so penetrated felt his limbs fill with courage and strength."

The archetypal Numen is the constant that germinates the seeds for future generations, whereas the individual or persona is the mutable and contingent aspect, the impermanent accessory of being. The vehicle to best preserve and propagate the archetypal Numen is the Stirpes.

In the ancient Roman Republic, the *tria nomina* was a naming convention used by the Romans and other peoples of Italy. The system of nomenclature differed from that used by other cultures in Europe and the Mediterranean, consisting of a combination of personal and family names. The names developed as part of this system became a defining characteristic of Roman civilization. However, a markedly different system of nomenclature arose in Italy, where the personal name was joined by a hereditary surname. Over time, this binomial system expanded to include additional names and designations. The most important of these names was the *nomen gentilicium*,

---

[22] Giammaria, *Da gli Atti degli Corpo dei Pari*, Edizioni Alkaest.

or simply *nomen*, a hereditary surname that identified a person as a member of a distinct gens or Stirpes. For example, with Gaius Julius Caesar, the 'Julius' refers to the iulius tribe, descended from the Trojan hero and progeny of Venus. In written form, the nomen was usually followed by a filiation, indicating the personal name of an individual's father, and sometimes the name of the mother or other antecedents. Towards the end of the Roman Republic, over the course of six centuries, as Roman institutions and social structures gradually fell away, the need to distinguish between *nomina* and *cognomina* likewise vanished. By the end of the seventh century, the people of Italy and western Europe had reverted to single names. But many of the names that had originated as part of the tria nomina were adapted to this usage, and survived into modern times. From the earliest period it was common to both the Indo-European speaking Italic peoples and the Etruscans. The historian Livy relates the adoption of Silvius as a nomen by the kings of Alba Longa in honor of their ancestor, Silvius. As part of Rome's foundation myth, this statement indicates the antiquity of the period to which the Romans themselves ascribed the adoption of hereditary surnames.[23]

Commentaries on The Golden Verses of Pythagoras[24]

Then should you be separated from the body, and soar into the Aether, you will be imperishable, a divinity, a mortal no more – *The Golden Verses of Pythagoras*

---

[23] Anthony Ossa-Richardson, *From Servius to Frazer: The Golden Bough and its Transformations*.

[24] Florence Firth, *Commentaries on the Golden Verses of Pythagoras*.

To best complete the circle of an Italic or Italic-Olympian spirituality, one must examine the important documents attributed to Orphic, Bacchic, and Pythagorean traditions. The Neo-Platonic philosophers of the late classical era considered the Pythagorean poem known as the *Golden Verses* to be one of the classic texts from the founding period of philosophy. The *Verses* speak of the relationships between man and the sacred in the context of an Olympian eschatological vision presented in the poem. There remains four extant commentaries from the classical era, two in Greek written by Iamblichus and Hierocles, and two commentaries preserved in Arabic, attributed to Iamblichus and Proclus. The *Verses* describe contemplative virtues, whose aim is to make men into Heroes, by practicing the divine virtues. By following the divine precepts of contemplative virtues faithfully, man will become truly spiritual, overcoming death, gaining a knowledge of the gods and their higher intelligences. In their essence all beings are of one nature with the Father, and as they are conscious of Him will they carry out His will and design, to maintain the beauty and harmony of the universe, because it is innate and essential reality, born into them as part of their divine nature. Therefore, the precepts are constantly observed by the Heroes, who remain steadily conscious of the Divine Will, to the extent to which they understand and know God.

The Illustrious Heroes are the second or middle order of beings, and are turned ever towards God, though not always to the same extent. They are divided into three sub-divisions: (1) The Angels, or Ambassadors (being nearest to the Immortal Gods in their nature); (2) The Numens, or Spirits; and (3) The Heroes. The terrestrial daemons are the souls of men, beautified with truth and virtue as masters of Wisdom. They are "terrestrial", remaining on earth in order to guide and govern men. The best worship to be offered to these men (who resemble the Illustrious Heroes), is by obeying the Pythagorean precepts and the tradition they have set down in writing. This tradition gives the principles of truth and rules of virtue, as an immortal and paternal inheritance, to be preserved to all succeeding generations for the common good. To obey these, and live accordingly, is the truest reverence that can be done to them.

The Pythagorean precepts followed and practiced by men – are to be reverenced as leading to the greatest strength and stability of character. And if man would reverence the precepts, then must he do all in his power to understand the laws that govern this universe, and endeavor to preserve harmony and order in all things. The Deliverance of the Soul is accomplished by The Purifications and is divided into two parts, one concerning itself with the physical body, and the other with the "luminous body" that makes use of their own soul, or essence, for to see and know this is to be freed from all evils. All the Purifications must be accomplished if man is to become free. It is to be noted that they deal with (1) the body, (2) the emotions and lower mind, and (3) the higher mind.[25]

Book six of the *Aeneid* recounts the hero Aeneas' journey down through the underworld with a prophetess called the Sibyl, and where the spirit of his father Anchises foretells his destiny as the founder of Rome and its Empire. This book has garnered great attention from scholars and the public alike, with respect to the interpretation of the ancient source of wisdom concerning Aeneas, the Golden Bough and his descent into the otherworld.

Maurus Servius Honoratus (Servius)[26] was a late fourth-century grammarian, with the reputation of being one of the most learned men of his generation in Italy; he

[25] Florence Firth, *Commentaries on the Golden Verses of Pythagoras.*
26 Anthony Ossa-Richardson, *From Servius to Frazer: The Golden*

was the author of a series of highly regarded commentaries on the internal meaning of the works of *Virgil*.

It was Servius' reference to the priesthood of Diana at Nemi that later set Frazer on his own voyage, to discern the true meaning of that myth. In addition to providing this information, Servius indulges in an allegorical reading of the Bough as the 'Pythagorean letter'. We know that Pythagoras of Samos divided human life according to the letter Y, that is, because the first age is unformed, given either to vices or to virtues, and that the fork of the letter Y begins with youth, at which time men follow either vice (the left path) or virtues (the right path). (Servius, *Commentarii*, pp.30-31.)

A century earlier, Lactantius had cited the letter as a common visualization technique useful in explaining ethical teachings, only to object that it fell short of the truth, "for the 'fork' occurs not during life, but at the moment of death, when a man's soul will go either to heaven or to hell" (Lactantius, *Divinae institutiones*, V1.3.5-10).

It is tempting to suggest that Servius conceived of the Y-shaped Bough as being "appropriately dedicated at the point where its bearer turned to the right along the path of virtue." However, the link remains implicit: Servius does allude to the Bough's function in the 'sacra Proserpinae' or death-offering, re-calling the circumstances of Prosperina's own capture by Hades: "[R]amus enim necesse erat ut et unius causa esset interitus ... et ad sacra Proserpinae accedere nisi sublato ramo non poterat..." (For the Bough was necessarily the cause of someone's death ... and he could not approach the holy places [Sacra, alternatively 'worship'] of Proserpina unless the Bough had been plucked).

Bough and its Transformations.

The association of the Golden Bough with the death of the hero who has it in his possession, is consistent with the metamorphosis or transformation which the initiate undergoes in his passage from the profane to the sacred. The initiate is truly reborn, purified of profane attachments and accretions, when his old self has died. Therefore, there are two noteworthy aspects of Servius' reading of the Bough. Firstly, it uses the image to reinforce a traditional point of ethics; and secondly, it augments the Bough's metaphorical resonances within the structure of *Aeneid* VI.

Within the scheme of the sixth book, the Golden Bough plays a special part, as the poet explains: "[*N*] *on antea discitur cognitio secretorum, nisi quis ramum decerpserit au-reum, id est doctrinae atque litterarum discatur studium. Ramum enim aureum pro scientia posuimus* ..." (There is no acquisition of secrets before one has plucked the Golden Bough, that is, until one has pursued a study of learning and literature. For the Golden Bough represents knowledge [Scientia]).

In the *Aeneid*, the Neo-Platonic doctrine of the soul's imprisonment in the body is fully articulated. The descent of the human soul into the body is also paralleled in *Aeneid* VI by the hero's own katabasis, which is an allegory for metaphysical 'descent', the progress towards philosophical wisdom.

Marsilio Ficino, meanwhile, in a recently-published excerpt from his *The Philebus Commentary*, digresses on a short interpretation of the katabasis: "*Aeneas, dum divinum ab oraculo auxilium imploraret, divina clementia impetravit ut ramum aureum sortiretur, mentis videlicet lumen infusum ab alto, quo perspicue tutoque posset per obscuras rerum latebras penetrare.*"

> When Aeneas ... became exhausted and implored divine help from the oracle, he was permitted by divine mercy to be allotted the Golden Bough (that is, the light of reason [mens] poured in from above), with which he could penetrate into the obscure retreats of things with clarity and safety.[27]

The commentary was written around 1491-92, and published in 1496. Proserpina's, capture by Hades represents the trapping of the ethereal spirit or life-force under the earth. *The Golden Bough*, by which the hero descends to Proserpina and safely returns, is interpreted as the initiatic art of harnessing this natural power.

The initiatic art consists of the effective passage from one state of being to another. Symbolized by the Ouroborous (snake swallowing its tale) that represents the initiatic process of journeying inward to exit outward. In the Italic tradition, initiation is best symbolized by the Magic Door, which the ancient Romans revered under the patronage of Janus, who presides over safe passage through gateways. For this reason, in the Western calendar, the first month of the year is called January in homage of the deity Janus who presides over the auspicious passage from the old to the new year, and also from the mundane to the magical.

For the 17th century British author, Francis Beaumont, this descent and vision of the Elysian Fields, a 'divine Institution of the Sibyl', is necessary for Aeneas before he becomes the founder of the Empire. The Bough is explained as 'that divine Spirit, which must be his passport to the Elysian fields', and its color is interpreted thus: "Gold, for that is a pure and incorruptible metal, and the

---

[27] Marsilio Ficino, *The Philebus Commentary*, ed. and tr. Michael J. B. Allen (Berkeley, Los Angeles, and London: University of California Press, 1975.

most ductile and extendible of all bodies, and in its color resembles the glorious Lights of Heaven, it terminating also the desires of man, was made by the ancients the sacred type of the divine, or of that divine nature diffus'd through the world ..."

In a later work, Beaumont makes a definite claim about Virgil's historical intentions. He returns to *Aeneid* VI in his essay on the ancient Sibyls, forming the second chapter of his 1724 *Gleanings of Antiquities*. Here, he reads the katabasis as a deliberate allegorical exposition of Virgil's own spiritual initiation: "Now these Verses manifestly show, that some Sibyl had led Virgil through the subterranean regions, as the Sibyl had carried Aeneas, and other Heroes, thither." Beaumont admits that "'the Mysteries of the Gentiles were consonant to our faith concerning God".

The traditional, Platonic exegesis of Bernard and Ficino have syncretized classical philosophy and contemporary religiosity, interpreting the katabasis as an occult descent towards sapientia, without any reference to authorial intent. We find a very similar occult descent, only now the allegory is grounded in Virgil's design; the syncretism, meanwhile, has been refashioned as a harmonization of historically discrete metaphysical systems. The change is subtle but profound.

The Bough reads variously as a "natural symbol of that visionary power granted by heaven to those whose eyes 'piercing in the quest' are to explore the viewless places of earth," as a "symbol of the transition from death to life", and as a "symbol of the power that is in [the voyager] of life and faith."

On Orphic and Bacchic Initiation

> Courage, brandish the warlike Thyrsus, and perform deeds worthy of the Aether, since the immortal Palace of Zeus will not receive you without hard work, and the seasons will not open the gates of Olympus, if first you don't engage in battle. – Zosimos of Panopolis, Grandfather of Panapoli, *Le Dionysian*, Song 13, 21-24

The goal of initiation, is not to be "initiated" but to be reborn and renewed, so the soul can resurge and blossom. And yet the Orphic-Bacchic (Dionysian) initiation helps to understand what it means to bring to light the initiate's base nature. The myth teaches that Dionysus was born twice, firstly as a son of Jupiter and Proserpine. Afterwards the Titans dismembered him and he was reborn, entrusted to Semele before the king of the gods kept him in his thigh. The Titans were persecuted, for their blood mixed with the Dionysian echo, the last generation of humans was born, that of the Iron Age. The goal of the initiation is precisely to extricate that Titanic account, to get rid of an obscure residue, and finally to be similar to the Gods. The Dionysian initiation, by analogy, repeats the luminescent rituals of the Sun, which in turn symbolizes the supreme intelligence from which it descends to the world of the senses. Then there will be no orthodoxy, no totalitarian hallucination, but the *ritus* (equivalent of the Sanskrit *Rta*, which means "cosmic order"). This act frees all from the desert of titanism propagated by Typhoon, the enemy of the divine and man.

In the museums of Southern Italy, texts engraved on small gold plates reside, that provide an extraordinary source of information on what the Greeks and Romans thought of the afterlife, and how they believed they could influence it. These texts, dating back to a period from the fifth century BC until the second century AD, belonged to those who had been initiated into the mysteries of Dionysus and Orpheus. The gold plates found in the graves of the initiates to Dionysus, describe Orphic precepts for the afterlife that spread across the Mediterranean, with the majority found in the Magna Graecia area of Southern Italy.

The Gold tablets, found next to the remains of the initiates, lay down the instructions for initiates to journey into the afterlife. The instructions indicate a map or path to follow. The initiate will be reborn in human form and therefore mortal, he will know a new life, and will continue in the circle of incarnations, to the point of completely purifying himself. Those who have already made their own *palingenesis* in existence, through rites that cancel the previous stains accompanied by inadequate conduct, will have to resist the thirst and go further. At a certain point they will see the source of Mnemosyne and can then drink, receiving refreshment without erasing the past. He can also reincarnate if necessary, but the next existence will be the last and will be punctuated by the awareness of past experiences: it is the path of memory, that leads to the guardians of the threshold, the custodians of the Elysian Fields. To proceed further, one must demonstrate their successful transformation with the simple presence of one's own profound being, and it will be necessary to recite words of passage, and then proceed upwards towards complete divinization.[28]

The following text is from the grave of a woman in Calabria, c. 400 BC:

> This is the work of Memory, when you are about to die
> Down to the well-built house of Hades. There is a

---

[28] Fritz Graff, *Ritual Texts for the Afterlife: Orpheus and the Bacchic Gold Tablets*, Routledge.

spring at the right side,

And standing by it a white cypress.

Descending to it, the souls of the dead refresh themselves.

Do not even go near this spring!

Ahead you will find from the Lake of Memory,

Cold water pouring forth, there are guards before it.

They will ask you, with astute wisdom,

What you are seeking in the darkness of murky Hades.

Say, "I am a son of Earth and the starry Sky,

I am parched with thirst and am dying; but quickly grant me

Cold water from the Lake of Memory to drink."

And they will grant you to drink form the Lake of Memory.

And you, too, having drunk will go along the sacred road on which the other

Glorious initiates and *bacchoi* travel.[29]

"I am a child of earth and starry heaven, but my race is of heaven alone".[30]

---

[29] Fritz Graff, *Ritual Texts for the Afterlife: Orpheus and the Bacchic Gold Tablets*, Routeledge.

[30] Alberto Bernabe, *Instructions for the Netherworld: The Orphic Gold Tablets*, Brill Academic Publication.

APPENDIX

The Influence of Giuliano Kremmerz on the UR Group

The impact of Kremmerz's teachings on Hermeticism and magic in Italy is both vast and profound. Not only did Kremmerz and his school, the Myriam, offer a contemporary and living example of initiation, they also provided a complete practice, with an indigenous rooted tradition, a sophisticated school of teachings, and an effective praxis that included Isisian and Osirian vectors for self-realization. We know from documents that have recently come to light that Evola not only sought initiation into the Myriam, but also maintained contact with members of the Myriam and the Grand Egyptian Order, such as Giovanni Bonnabitocala (head of the Vergil Academy of the Myriam Rome), Father Francesco Oliva and Antonio de Santis (Primo Sole and Nilius), and Francesco Proto da Atrani (Apro) of the Grand Egyptian Order. The private letters detailing the correspondence between Father Oliva and Evola remain reserved in private archives of the Myriam's present day offshoots.

After the UR experience, Kremmerz's influence continued, especially on Evola's more esoteric writings including the *Hermetic Tradition, Mask and Face of*

Contemporary Spiritualism, and the *Cinnabar Path*. In the *Metaphysics of Sex*, there is a chapter devoted to "Sex in the Domain of Initiations and Magic," where Evola describes in detail the doctrine of "Eros and the Mysteries of Love" as practiced by the Myriam and applied through the techniques of Fire Magic.

There are analogies between the Myriam, the collective chain of the sodality, and the Christian mystical theology of the Virgin Mary or Theotokos (Mother of God), as the archetypal woman, personification of the church and bestower of supernatural life. Likewise, the path of Venus is aroused by lighting a psychic flame through the practice of fire magic, in a harmonious and loving relationship to the extent that the woman becomes a powerful medium, aiding the Hermetic practitioner. The female essentially provides the fluid to arouse and magnetize the will, bringing it to a state of androgyny. The magus cannot engage in relations unless he possesses his fluidic opposite in a woman, thus the necessity of a special complement or polarity is a requisite for strong erotic magnetism. Fire magic is ignited when "Love begins to acquire a holy character that puts the human soul into a state of Mag or trance."

What follows next are passages taken from Kremmerz's works which are almost all out of print or unobtainable. They have been recompiled with slight modifications.

*****

Our purity, fully understood, is the conscious and unalterable neutrality of consciousness. Every manifestation of hate and every love, I would say every interest of the Hermetic operator, in the successful outcome of the desired thing, renders useless, annuls, destroys the expected result.

In the full physical and mental equilibrium, in a regime of sober life, without efforts, silently observing, realizing the vanity of the word, the propitious development of Hermetic intelligence is realized.

Mentally detach yourself, from the surrounding environment, as from something that should not and cannot bother you. Say: the unrighteous will not affect my equilibrium. For the idea of the most perfect person assumes the image of the completely Integrated: The perfect man is neither entirely body or spirit, but the integration of the powers of the spirit in the body that nourishes it and serves as the basis for its manifestation, in a constant equilibrium that prevents the excess of either one or the other factors.

In physical world, use the will to obtain anything and to abstain from anything. By submitting life to a sober regimen, the body is strengthened. If you are sick, fast. Address this refrain to passions and desires. Passions are sufferings for desires not achieved or not satisfied enough. Desire with sobriety, and when desire exceeds, be righteous. That which is most distant from power, is glutinous desires.

A Master must be superior to good and evil, because from his neutrality to one or the other effect depends his continuous balanced state, such as to develop internal powers and to use them in every sense. Each operation bears the status of the imbalance or imbalance of the operator.

You are yourself the laboratory, and it is necessary that you see clearly as in the light of the sun. Reflect on your actions and meditate on them. The characteristics, the impulsive ones, those that preserve their regularity, will deprive you of your ancient being, your forgotten history and what you have been. Get into the habit of frequently examining your conscience.

Being sincere with yourself is necessary, and it is the most difficult thing to achieve.

Your thought acts directly on the body and with sufficient training you will dispose of it entirely. Do not be afraid of infections, infirmities, and disturbances of any kind. Among weaker constitutions the will is imagined, among those most accustomed it is simply affirmed. Then you will no longer need "suggestions"; it will be enough for you to will with confidence, like the virtuoso who has mastered an instrument.

Hermetic practice has the tendency to make the integrative faculty of the human intellect absolute master of the animal shell, to make it an obedient servant and ready to serve the psychodynamic authority that is in us. Purified of any obstacle to the free exercise of the intelligent will: free from needing.

With man being conceived as analogous to the cosmos, magic has as the basis of its precepts the analogical laws of things and acts that are performed. For example, lavender is an analogical symbol of the virtue of water that cleanses the bath stone; that of fasting, is analogous to the liberation from obstructions; that of chastity, to a state of freedom, and not of concupiscent passion, that is of suffering.

Wash yourself in order that with this act that your hands not only clean your body and their outward senses, but above all the hidden essence that has received impure impressions during the day. If by prudence you practice fasting during the full moon, eating only once – because you know that on the first day of its appearance the moon is virginal, innocent and pure analogically to the lunar or astral body of man.

A realization, whether above or below, is an act of love: both for good and for evil: for what brings usefulness and for what brings harm. Any idea of personal benefit, muddies and arrests – whether of moral or material compensation; it's all the same. If a lover "prays" for his woman, he will not realize anything if he does not convert his love as a lover into that of a mother who sacrifices herself for her child.

This love is called Beatrice, because it is Light, Purity, Bliss. It is not an art and it is not a science. It is a spirit that announces Hermes, like Dawn announces the Sun. It is necessary to invoke it. If it comes, do not distance it, because it will not come back. If it comes receive it. Whoever you love will be taken by the same love and if it is more perfect it will give you everything you ask of its spirit. This is the first small key.

Such love ceases to be necessarily linked to a particular being. On the contrary, we believe that the allusion to the aforementioned love between two people has above all the purpose of making it understood, by analogy, of what state it is: a state that in magic must be able to evoke itself without supporting it and binding it to anything.

Hermetic prayer, is an act of concrete fluidification of the will. Formulate the idea, and desire its realization, that is prayer. Prayer, hermetically and an act of concrete fluidization of the will. Formulate the idea, and desire[1] its realization. The imagination of things well defined, pictorial, minute, chiseled in the most fine and defined

---
[1] It is evident here that the sort of "desire" evoked is different in order from that, which Kremmerz himself, in conformance with his magical teaching, says paralyzes realization.

details, and willing in act, and creation. To conceive, to imagine, to withdraw the idea well, then to feel in the state of truth, in agreement. and in conscience, with the thought thing, and act of will, whether the word expresses the volitional thought, and that it does not express it. The will is perfect when the idea is shaped and the idea lived in consciousness. Peace between imagined idea and conscience, willingness in action, love that intervenes and fruitful.

In the integrated consciousness, with the profound will, beyond any influence of the environment, belief or passion, the Hermetic power manifests itself spontaneously, effortlessly, through the only imaginative act. The imagination and the instrument of creation of integrated consciences. It is enough to create a form conceived in this inner condition, so that the form is realized, not as a result of an effort, but as that of a state of being independent and intimate, which knows no obstacles. The conception, in magic, is a flash, a lightning operation that implies perfect education both of the physical body and of the mental one. So: close your eyes, create an image and aim it. In the dark, you will see a view that is not that sensitive. Let more people in the same way close their eyes and open their inner vision – then the communion with light is established by relationship.

The relationship between the astral vibrations perceived by the individual forms the astral current, which in time you must learn to master.

Hermes conceives the mental motion outside of the body, surface, or space: free motion in an intellectual environment without dimensions, or that includes all dimensions. The human mind hermetically penetrated in this function, portrays a divine virtue that turns into miraculous powers.

All that is thought in the astral realm, can be realized in act: things that are hermetically thought are real facts, because they become real outcomes. Enter in contact with the world beyond, and actively engage in this realm to realize outcomes. or effects, in real life.

Therefore, the purpose is precisely to:

reduce man to the state of ether;
reduce ether to a state of fire;
reduce the evil that comes in contact through the integrated purifying movement.
The Symbols: Hermes who loves Venus
The Name: Fire Magic, or eonic magic
The Mystery: The initiate closed in the deep darkness of his hood
The Outcome: the Hermaphrodite, the indissoluble unity of the complementaries
The Sign: The open palmed hand – the Flame
The Means: Silence.

AUTHOR & ARTIST BIOGRAPHY

Author

David Pantano is an independent researcher in Eastern and Western inner traditions.

Illustrator

Josef Stefanka is a multi-disciplined artist based in surrealistic styles of expression.

www.ingramcontent.com/pod-product-compliance
Lightning Source LLC
Chambersburg PA
CBHW031643170426
43195CB00035B/407